The Boys Are Kissing

Zak Zarafshan

T0027226

methuen | drama

LONDON • NEW YORK • OXFORD • NEW DELHI • SYDNEY

METHUEN DRAMA
Bloomsbury Publishing Plc
50 Bedford Square, London, WC1B 3DP, UK
1385 Broadway, New York, NY 10018, USA
29 Earlsfort Terrace, Dublin 2, Ireland

BLOOMSBURY, METHUEN DRAMA and the Methuen
Drama logo are trademarks of Bloomsbury Publishing Plc

First published in Great Britain 2023

Cover design: Steph Pyne

A catalogue record for this book is available from the British Library.

A catalog record for this book is available from the Library of Congress.

ISBN: PB: 978-1-3504-1162-3
ePDF: 978-1-3504-1163-0
eBook: 978-1-3504-1164-7

Series: Modern Plays

Typeset by Mark Heslington Ltd, Scarborough, North Yorkshire

To find out more about our authors and books visit
www.bloomsbury.com and sign up for our newsletters.

The Boys Are Kissing

By Zak Zarafshan

The Boys Are Kissing was first performed at
Theatre503, London, on 17 January 2023.

The Boys Are Kissing

By Zak Zarafshan

CAST

Amira Rasheed-Owen – Seyan Sarvan
Chloe Rasheed-Owen – Eleanor Wyld
Sarah O'Connell – Amy McAllister
Matt O'Connell – Philip Coreia
Cherub One – Shane Convery
Cherub Two – Kishore Walker

CREATIVE TEAM

Director – Lisa Spirling
Designer – Aldo Vazquez
Lighting Designer – Jodie Underwood
Sound Designer – Calum Perrin
Movement Director – Mateus Daniel
Associate Director – Len Gwyn
Costume Supervisor – Malena Arcucci
Casting Director – Emily Jones
Production Manager – Tabitha Piggott
Stage Manager – Summer Keeling
Rehearsal Room Stage Manager – Rose Hockaday
Placement Assistant Stage Manager – Rebecca Elsey
Sound Programmer/Access Support – Wilkie Morrison
Dialect Coach – Marianne Samuels
Producer – Ceri Lothian
Assistant Producer – Tsipora St. Clair Knights
PR – Nancy Poole

Amira Rasheed-Owen – Seyan Sarvan

Seyan's stage credits include: *Hercuba Birangona* (Kali Theatre Company); *Moonfleece* (Pleasance Theatre); *Off* (Arcola); *Skeen* (Stockwell Playhouse); *The Most Incredible Nothing* (Battersea Arts Centre); *1984* (Lyric Hammersmith Theatre).

Television credits include: *The Baby* (HBO); *It's A Sin* (Studio Canal); *Krypton* (Warner Bros).

Film credits include: *Things We Never Said* (BFI & Wild Swim); *Spin State* (React Films); *51 States* (BFI).

Chloe Rasheed-Owen – Eleanor Wyld

Theatre includes: *Pinocchio* (Unicorn); *The Merchant Of Venice* (The Globe/Sam Wanamaker Playhouse); *Leopoldstadt* (Wyndham's Theatre); *The Ballad Of Corona V* (Big House Theatre); *Don Quixote* (RSC Stratford/Garrick Theatre); *About Leo* (Jermyn Street); *Doctor Faustus* (RSC); *Hamlet* (RSC – UK and USA Tour 2018); *Don Juan In Soho* (Wyndham's Theatre); *The Alchemist* (RSC); *After Electra* (Theatre Royal Plymouth/Tricycle Theatre); *Bedroom Farce/Separate Tables* (Salisbury Playhouse); *VISITORS* (Arcola Theatre/National Tour/Bush Theatre); *Unscorched* (Finborough Theatre); *Dances Of Death* (Gate Theatre); *The Astronaut's Chair* (Theatre Royal Plymouth); *Shiverman* (Theatre503); *His Teeth* (Only Connect); *Antigone* (Southwark Playhouse); *The Deep Blue Sea* (West Yorkshire Playhouse).

Television includes: *Trigonometry, Lovesick, #FINDTHEGIRL, Thirteen, Father Brown, Holby City, Doctors, Misfits, Black Mirror: The National Anthem, Casualty, Honest, You Can Choose Your Friends* and *Coronation Street.*

Film includes: *Bonobo, Johnny English Reborn, The Manual* and *Freestyle.*

Sarah O'Connell – Amy McAllister

Amy McAllister trained at the Guildhall School of Music and Drama.

Theatre includes: *Scorch* (Soho/World Tour); *The Noises* (Old Red Lion); *My Romantic History, Harriet Martineau Dreams Of Dancing, A Northern Odyssey* (Live Theatre); *Forever Yours, Mary-Lou* (Theatre Royal Bath); *Sons Without Fathers* (Arcola); *Hecuba* (RSC); *Shadow Of A Gunman* (Abbey Theatre).

TV/Film includes: *Breeders* (Sky/Avalon); *A Discovery Of Witches* (Sky/Bad Wolf); *There She Goes* (BBC/Merman); *Miss Scarlet And The Duke* (PBS/Element 8); *Witless* (BBC/Objective); *The Great Fire* (ITV); *Call The Midwife* (BBC/Neal Street); *Philomena* (BBC Films/Baby Cow).

Radio/Voiceover includes: *The Electricity Of Every Living Thing* (Audible); *Promises, The Van, The Snapper* (BBC); *Dora And The Lost City Of Gold* (Paramount/Nickelodeon); *Sherlock Holmes* (Audible); *Artemis Fowl* (Disney).

Amy is also a poet. She has won numerous poetry slams including the UK Anti-Slam, the Hammer & Tongue London Slam Championship, the UK Team Slam Finals at the Royal Albert Hall and the Great Northern Slam. Her debut collection *Are You As Single As That Cream?* is published by Burning Eye.

Matt O'Connell – Philip Coreia

Theatre credits include: *Much Ado About Nothing, Holy Warriors, Antony and Cleopatra, A Midsummer Night's Dream, Walks* (Shakespeare's Globe); *Othello* (ETT); *NT50* (NT Olivier); *The Pitman Painters* (NT/BKL); *Betrayal* (Derby Theatre); *The Herbal Bed* (Rose/Royal and Derngate); *Judgement Day* (Print Room); *The Syndicate* (Chichester Festival & Tour); *The History Boys* (Wyndham's, NT Lyttleton & Tour).

Screen credits include: *The War Below* (Vital); *Bliss!* (S&W); *The Hunters* (Lionsgate); *Jerk* (Roughcut/Primal); *Coronation Street, Lewis, Vera* (ITV); *Casualty, Doctors, Holby City* (BBC); *Atlantis* (Little Monster Films); *Inspector George Gently* (Company); *Hollyoaks* (Lime); *Canoe Man* (Dragonfly); *The Bill* (Talkback Thames).

Writing/Directing credits include: *Hyem* (Theatre503/Northern Stage); *The Invisible Man* (Northern Stage); *Yard Tales* (The Playground Theatre); *Frestonia* (St Mary's Drama).

Cherub One – Shane Convery

Irish actor Shane trained at the Royal Conservatoire of Scotland and graduated in 2017.

Theatre credits include: *Yeast Nation, Anyone Can Whistle* (Southwark Playhouse); *The Wizard Of Oz* (Selladoor Worldwide); *Sleepin' Cutie* (MacRoberts Arts Centre); *Safe Place* (Orán Mor/Traverse Theatre Edinburgh); *Chess* (RCS/Festival Theatre Edinburgh).

Television credits include: *Nolly* (ITV); *The B Team, Almost Never* (Series 2) (BBC); *Fairview Park* (BFI).

Cherub Two – Kishore Walker

Kishore trained at Guildhall School of Music and Drama. This is his professional debut.

Television credits include *Doctors* (BBC).

Writer – Zak Zarafshan

Zak Zarafshan is a British-Iranian playwright and screenwriter from the East Midlands, based in London. His debut play, *The Boys Are Kissing*, was developed as part of Theatre503's Writers In Residence scheme, the 503Five.

He was previously a part of the Soho Theatre Writers' Lab, Tamasha Playwrights Group, and was shortlisted for Channel 4's 4Stories scheme.

Director – Lisa Spirling

Lisa Spirling has been the Artistic Director and Chief Executive of Theatre503 London since 2016. She is the Creative Associate of Eleanor Lloyd Productions. Previously she was the coordinator of the JMK Trust Regional Director's Programme and a founder of Buckle for Dust Theatre Company.

Productions include: *Wagatha Christie* (West End, ELP Productions); *Milk & Gall*, *Wolfie*, *In Event Of Moone Disaster* (Theatre503); *Jumpy* (Theatr Clwyd); *Describe The Night*, *Ken*, *Pine*, *Deposit*, *Fault Lines*, *I Know How I Feel About Eve* (Hampstead Theatre); *Donkeys' Years* and *HERE* (Rose Theatre); *Hundreds & Thousands* (Buckle For Dust / English Touring Theatre / Soho Theatre); *Cotton Wool* (Buckle for Dust / Theatre503).

Designer – Aldo Vazquez

Aldo is a Mexican set and costume designer based in the UK. He trained at Bristol Old Vic Theatre School with an MA in Theatre Design, and a BA in Visual Arts from the UNAM/ENAP, Mexico City. He has worked both in Mexico and the UK collaborating with international directors and actors from Argentina, Canada, China, Mexico, USA, UK and Switzerland.

In the UK he designed *Moreno* written by Pravin Wilkins and directed by Nancy Medina (Theatre503, 2022). Since 2020 he has worked on several graduating shows for Bristol Old Vic Theatre School and Bristol School of Acting with directors including Nancy Medina, Tom Morris, Aaron Parsons, Donaccadh O'Briain and Derek Bond. Alongside his work in theatre he designed the costumes for the reopening of Battersea Power Station.

In Mexico he has designed for a variety of different projects, as well as being part of three of the annual Festival Internacional de Teatro Universitario, and designed for the Swiss-Mexico Dramafest festival. He has collaborated with the following directors: Enrique Singer, Teatro ojo, Angélica Rogel, Paula Zelaya, Emiliano Dionisi, He Hao, Francine Alepin and Mathieu Bertolet.

Lighting Designer – Jodie Underwood

Jodie Underwood is a lighting designer with work spanning theatre, opera and dance. After graduating from RADA with a first class honours, she launched into a career in lighting design and associating. Jo is particularly interested in working with new writing, and more unconventional theatrical forms. Their credits include: *Horse Play* (dir. Andrew Beckett); *The Paul Taylor Mills Summer Rep* (Paul Taylor Mills); *The Haunting Of Susan A, La Boheme* (dir. Mark Ravenhill); *Dirty Corset* (Bang Average Theatre); *Us, Aphiemi & The Friday Freedom Fighters* (Pathway Theatre); *The Man Who Though He Knew Too Much* (Voloz Collective); *Dick Whittington!* (The Big Tiny Theatre); *La Princess De Trebizonde* (New Sussex Opera); *Selected Recordings Of Us* (Undone Theatre). Their associate LD credits include *Ride* (Charing Cross, LD Jamie Platt); *Dick Whittington: A New Dick In Town!* (Above The Stag, LD Jamie Platt) and *Catching Comets* (Ransack Theatre, LD Matt Leventhall).

Sound Designer – Calum Perrin

Calum Perrin works across visual art, theatre, music and radio. They explore themes of disability, sensory experience and domesticity, as well as the relationship between documentary processes and artistic practice. Calum has worked with organisations including BBC Radio 3 and 4, BBC Sounds, Audible, Paraorchestra, VICE, Donmar Warehouse, The Yard and Drake Music. They were the artist in residence at the Museum of the Home in 2021.

Movement Director – Mateus Daniel

Mateus Daniel is a movement director and performer who studied Physical Theatre at East 15 Acting School and has worked with Street Circus Collective (The Roundhouse), The Pappy Show, Talawa Theatre Company and Upswing. His movement director credits include *Passion Fruit* (New Diorama); *Definitely Fine Theatre* (The Curve); *Human Nurture* (Theatre Peckham and tour), and was recently nominated for Best Choreographer at the BBTAs.

Associate Director – Len Gwyn

Len Gwyn works as a drag king, performance maker, musician, comedian, actor and facilitator from Cardiff, based in London.

Since becoming a finalist of Europe's biggest drag king competition, *Man Up*, in 2016, Len has been kinging in alternative cabaret lineups at iconic queer venues like the Royal Vauxhall Tavern, The Glory, and Bethnal Green Working Men's Club, as well as at Soho Theatre, Southbank Centre, the Clapham Grand and the

Hackney Empire. In 2018 Len put kings on a national platform when they sang in drag on BBC1's *All Together Now*. They are now a freelance teacher of drag and cabaret, running courses, showcases, open mic nights and judging competitions. Alongside this, Len performs as a genderqueer actor and musician, mostly for fringe theatre productions. As a voiceover artist, they have worked in comedy dramas with BBC Radio Wales, Audible and podcast *Victoriocity*. Len is a lover of the unruly and improvised at the shows they host and perform in. Their work is about querying and challenging the gender binary through singing, pointing, laughing and winking.

Costume Supervisor – Malena Arcucci

Born and raised in Buenos Aires, Argentina, Malena Arcucci is a theatre designer and costume supervisor based in London. She is co-artistic director of Mariana Malena Theatre Company.

Design credits include: *The Bit Players* (Southwark Playhouse); *Friday Night Love Poem* (Zoo Venues Edinburgh); *Point Of No Return* (Actor's Centre); *La Llorona* (Dance City Newcastle); *The Two Of Us* (Theatre Deli); *Playing Latinx* (Camden's People's Theatre) and various productions in Buenos Aires, Argentina.

Associate Designer credits include: *Dear Elizabeth* (The Gate); *Chiaroscuro* (Bush Theatre); *Thebes Land* and *Tamburlaine* (Arcola Theatre).

Costume Supervisor and Maker credits include: *Blues For An Alabama Sky* (as assistant, National Theatre); *The Cherry Orchard* (The Yard and HOME); *Chasing Hares* (Young Vic); *House Of Ife* (Bush Theatre); *Lotus Beauty* (Hampstead Theatre); *Milk And Gall*, *Moreno* (Theatre503); *The Phantom Of The Opera* (Her Majesty's Theatre); and *Raya* (Hampstead Theatre) amongst others.

Casting Director – Emily Jones

Emily is an experienced casting director for theatre, film and television.

Theatre casting includes: *Seeds* (Pleasance Theatre); *Never Not Once* (Park Theatre); *Gaslight* (Watford Palace); *Much Ado About Nothing* (Opera Dubai); *Blue Orange* (Birmingham Rep); *Our Lady Of Kibeho* (Northampton); *Henry V* (Barn Theatre); *Parents' Evening*, *The Play About My Dad* (Jermyn Street Theatre); *Beirut, World Enough, Time*, *The Keeper Of Infinite Space* (Park Theatre); *Gulliver Returns* (Edinburgh Festival & UK Tour); *Our Blue Heaven* (New Wolsey Theatre); *The Devil With The Blue Dress* (Bunker Theatre); *Broken Glass* (Watford Palace); *Child Of The Divide* (Bhuchar Boulevard); *Powerplay* (Hampton Court Palace); *Orca* (Southwark Playhouse); *Donkey Heart* (Trafalgar Studios/Old Red Lion); *Coolatully*, *The Hard Man*, *Unscorched* (Finborough Theatre).

Film & TV credits include: *Finding Clive* (Revolution Films/Deva Films); *Doctors* (BBC); *Beauty* (Moolmore Films); *What Happened To Evie* (French Fancy Productions); *Practice* (Deva Films); *Collection Only* (Constant Productions).

Production Manager – Tabitha Piggott

Tabitha Piggott is a production manager for stage working in theatre and opera, with a particular passion for new writing. She studied Production and Technical Arts at LAMDA as a Leverhulme Arts Scholar, and was production manager on Papatango and Bush Theatre's Olivier Award-winning *Old Bridge* in 2021.

Credits include: *All Of Us*, *Barrier(s)*, *Connections 2022* (National Theatre); *Only An Octave Apart* (Wilton's Music Hall); *Paradise Now!*, *Favour*, *Red Pitch*, *Old Bridge*, *Overflow* (Bush Theatre); *Fefu And Her Friends* (Tobacco Factory Theatres); *Raising Icarus* (Birmingham Rep); *The Winner's Curse*, *The 4th Country* (Park Theatre); *The Boys Are Kissing*, *Moreno* (Theatre503); *The Dancing Master* (Buxton Opera House).

Stage Manager – Summer Keeling

Recent credits include: *The Grotto* (Drayton Arms Theatre); *The Light Trail*, *The Moors*, *Hand Of God* (The Hope Theatre); *The Haunting Of Susan A* (King's Head Theatre); *Til Death Do Us Part* (Theatre503); *Ghosts Of The Titanic* (Park 90); *Instructions For A Teenage Armageddon* (Southwark Playhouse); *Thrill Me: The Leopold And Loeb Story* (Jermyn Street Theatre); *21 Round For Christmas*, *Darling*, *Fever Pitch Mario!* (The Hope Theatre); *Mario! A Super Musical* (The Cockpit).

Summer trained at Mountview Academy of Theatre Arts in Theatre Production Arts (2017).

Rehearsal Room Stage Manager – Rose Hockaday

Rose Hockaday is a freelance stage manager based in London.

Theatre: *Age Is A Feeling*, *At Broken Bridge*, *No Particular Order* (Ellandar); *Volcano*, *Lately*, *Antigone*, *Spiderfly*, *Mites*, *Phoenix*, *Pops*, *The Ex-Boyfriend Yard Sale* (London & Toronto); *No Particular Order*, *Milk & Gall*, *Wolfie*, *Art Of Gaman* (Theatre503); *You Only Live Forever*, *In Tents And Purposes* (Viscera Theatre); *Timmy*, *Glitter Punch*, *Sophie*, *Ben And Other Problems*, *How To Survive A Post-Truth Apocalypse*, *They Built It. No One Came* and *Jericho Creek* (Fledgling Theatre).

Film: *Heaven Knows*, *Visitors*, *Ignite*, *Pomegranate*, *Wandering Eyes* and *Versions Of Us*, as well as music videos for the songs 'Phase Me Out', 'When You're Gone' and 'Saint' for artist VÉRITÉ.

Placement Assistant Stage Manager – Rebecca Elsey

Becca is currently training in Stage Management at the Royal Central School of Speech and Drama. They have a particular interest in children's theatre and the highlighting of queer stories. During training they have taken on the role of Assistant Stage Manager on productions such as *London Road*, *Duchess Of Malfi* and *The Castle*. They have also had the opportunity to stage manage *Call Me Mother Goose: A Drag Panto*, which toured primary schools in Oldham, and the play *Absolute Hell*. Becca is very excited and grateful to be a part of this project.

Sound Programmer/Access Support – Wilkie Morrison

Wilkie is a sound engineer, mixer, musician and music producer. He graduated from RADA in 2022 with a degree in Technical Theatre and Stage Management.

Theatre includes: Harper Lee's *To Kill A Mockingbird* (Gielgud Theatre 2022); *Anything Goes* (2022 UK Tour and Barbican); *Jack And The Beanstalk* (Hackney Empire 2021).

For Theatre503: *The Boys Are Kissing*, *Tapped*, freelance sound engineer for other productions.

Dialect Coach – Marianne Samuels

Marianne Samuels is a voice and dialect coach and specialist in the field of voice. She is company dialect coach for Stagebox, teaching professional young talent for stage and screen roles, and voice and text actors support for the Royal Shakespeare Company. Credits include: *The Clothes They Stood Up In*, *Private Peaceful*, *Moonlight* and *Magnolias*, *Boar* (Nottingham Playhouse); *Newark Newark* (Balloon Entertainment/UKGold); *A Christmas Carol* (RSC); *Journeys of Destiny* (Derby Theatre); *Acting Alone* (Derby Theatre and Nottingham Playhouse); *The Vagina Monologues* (Newark Palace Theatre); *Hundreds and Thousands* (Buckle for Dust/English Touring Company) and *Larkrise To Candleford* (Finborough Theatre). Marianne has taught voice and dialect at leading drama schools the Royal Central School of Speech and Drama, Birmingham Conservatoire Acting and Drama Studio London. Marianne runs Zen Voice & Body/ Zen Coaching Company.

THEATRE503

Theatre503 is at the forefront of identifying and nurturing new voices at the very start of their careers and launching them into the industry. They stage more early career playwrights than any other theatre in the world – with over 120 writers premiered each year from festivals of short pieces to full-length productions, resulting in employment for over 1,000 freelance artists through their year-round programme.

Theatre503 provides a diverse pipeline of talent resulting in modern classics like *The Mountaintop* by Katori Hall and *Rotterdam* by Jon Brittain – both Olivier Award winners – to future classics like Yasmin Joseph's *J'Ouvert*, winner of the 2020 James Tait Black Prize which transferred to the West End/BBC Arts, and *Wolfie* by Ross Willis, winner of the 2020 Writers Guild Award for Best New Play. Writers who began their creative life at Theatre503 are now writing for the likes of *The Crown*, *Succession*, *Doctor Who*, *Killing Eve* and *Normal People* and every single major subsidised theatre in the country now boasts a new play by a writer who started at Theatre503.

THEATRE503 TEAM

Artistic Director	Lisa Spirling
Interim Executive Director	Juliette Oakshett
Literary Manager	Steve Harper
Producer	Ceri Lothian
General Manager	Tash Berg
Carne Associate Director	Jade Lewis
Literary Associate	Lauretta Barrow
Trainee Assistant Producers	Catherine Moriarty, Tsipora St. Clair Knights
Marketing Officer	Millie Whittam
Administrator	Lizzie Akita
Development Coordinator	Heloise Gillingham

Theatre503 Board

Erica Whyman OBE (Chair)	Jack Tilbury
Celine Gagnon (Co-Vice Chair)	Luke Shires
Royce Bell (Co-Vice Chair)	Ollie Raggett
Eleanor Lloyd	Roy Williams OBE
Emma Rees	Zena Tuitt

Theatre503 would like to thank:

Callan McCarthy and all the team at Bloomsbury, Katie Bonna, Oliver Buckner, Hadeel Elshak, George Jones, Clare Lawrence Moody, Will Norris, Giles Smart.

This production was supported using public funding by the National Lottery through Arts Council England.

Theatre503's work would not be possible without the support of the following individuals, trusts and organisations:

We are particularly grateful to Philip and Christine Carne and the long-term support of The Carne Trust for our International Playwriting Award, the 503 Five and Carne Associate.

Share the Drama Patrons: Ali Taylor, Angela Hyde-Courtney, Berlin Associates, Cas & Philip Donald, David Baxter & Carol Rahn, DavidsonMorris Solicitors, Eilene Davidson, Eric Bensaude, Erica Whyman, Geraldine Sharpe-Newton, Ian Mill KC, Jack Tilbury/Plann, Jennifer Jacobs, Jenny Sheridan, Jill Segal, Joachim Fleury, Jon & NoraLee Sedmak, Liberty Oberlander, Marcus Markou & Dynamis, Marianne Badrichani, Mike Morfey, Nick Hern Books, Pam Alexander & Roger Booker, Patricia Hamzahee, Richard Bean, Robert O'Dowd, Sean Winnett, The Bell Family, The Bloor Family, Tim Roseman, Tim Willcox, Tom Gowans and all our 503Friends and Share the Drama supporters.

503Slate Supporters: Cas & Philip Donald, Concord Theatricals, Eilene Davidson, Gordon Bloor, Jean Doumanian, Kater Gordon, Kofi Owusu Bempah, Royce Bell.

Arts Council England Grants for the Arts, Backstage Trust, Battersea Power Station Foundation (Right to Write), Cockayne Grants for the Arts (503 Productions), Concord Theatricals (503 Playwriting Award), Garrick Charitable Trust, Noel Coward Foundation (Rapid Write Response), Theatres Trust, The Foyle Foundation, The Orseis Trust (503Five), Wandsworth Borough Council, Wimbledon Foundation (Five-O-Fresh).

Writer's Thanks

For my parents. Thank you.

I'd also like to thank Lisa Spirling, Steve Harper and Ceri Lothian at 503 for believing in me and scaling every mountain to make this play a reality. To my fellow 503Five, Jon Berry, Annie Jenkins, Benedict Lombe, Joel Tan, the whole cast and team who worked on the play, and everyone who contributed along the way. I'm eternally grateful to you all.

The Boys Are Kissing

Characters

Amira Rasheed-Owen, *late thirties, British-Pakistani.*
Chloe Rasheed-Owen, *late thirties, White-British.*
Sarah O'Connell, *late thirties, White-British.*
Matt O'Connell, *late thirties, White-British.*
Cherub One, *an omniscient, omnipotent, angel-like, winged cherub.*
Cherub Two, *as above.*
John O'Connell, *Matt's father, played by* **Cherub One**.
Guide, *a softly-spoken meditation guide, played by* **Cherub Two**.
Saima Rasheed, *Amira's mother, played by* **Cherub One**.
Louise, *a silly little bitch, played by* **Cherub Two**.
Officer One, *a police officer, played by* **Cherub One**.
Officer Two, *a police officer, played by* **Cherub Two**.
Lucas O'Connell, *late twenties, Sarah and Matt's son, played by* **Cherub One**.
Samir Rasheed-Owen, *late twenties, Chloe and Amira's son, played by* **Cherub Two**.

Notes on Text

A line break during dialogue indicates a renewing of speech.

An en-dash (–) denotes an interruption.

A forward slash (/) indicates talking through an interruption.

The set should indicate a split between two 'dimensions': the divine world of The Cherubs, ideally 'above' the stage or on another level, and that of the naturalistic world.

Whenever The Cherubs are on stage, the effects of their power on the world should be indicated theatrically, through lighting, music, etc. Where I have specific ideas on this it is indicated in the text, but these are all open to interpretation. Throughout, including when The Cherubs are playing other characters, their wings are always visible (except where specified otherwise), we always know it is them.

When The Cherubs are narrating the scenes flow into each other, the other characters appear on stage as needed, scene transitions should be fluid.

Act One

The suggestion of a domestic setting, living room decor, but abstract and as if open to the sky, perhaps a dual staircase leading up to the heavens. The set is exaggerated and camp, maybe everything is pink or lilac – the wood panelling, the rug, the sofas.

Sarah *surveys the room in awe, while* **Matt** *anxiously hovers around the perimeter.* **Amira,** *with a noticeable baby bump, punches away at her emails on her phone.* **Chloe** *flurries back and forth setting the table for tea.*

Chloe   Well that's the thing, you see, we'd have never been able to afford a place like this in London.

Sarah   Not with a garden like that, I mean, so mature and . . . so much space.

Chloe   Exactly.

Matt *peers out of a window in the corner.*

Sarah   I always think with these city-dwellers, where do their kids play?

Chloe   Exactly what I tell Amira. You can't live like this in the city.

Sarah   Well I for one don't want my kids fiddling with syringes and getting stabbed on the school run.

Amira   I didn't grow up fiddling with syringes or getting stabbed.

Chloe   Well you wouldn't in Wimbledon would you?

Sarah   I mean, obviously I see the benefits of diversity but if you have to be a millionaire to buy a house how diverse can it really be?

Amira *rolls her eyes.*

Sarah   Matt, why are you lurking over there by the window?

Matt   Oh, I'm just
I'm just –

Amira   You're looking very tense, Matt. Is something the matter?

Matt   Are you sure they're alright out there?

Amira   Why wouldn't they be?

Matt   They're on the trampoline.

Amira   Yes?

Matt   Are you sure they should
Should someone not –

Chloe   The box did actually say 'to be used under direct supervision'.

Amira   Nobody follows what it says on the box.

Matt   But if that's what the box says?

Amira   I think nine is old enough for them to be unsupervised.

Matt   Are you sure? Are you sure it's safe?

Chloe   There's a safety net Matt. There's no way they can fall off.

Matt   Maybe I should go out and keep watch.

Sarah   It's going to be pretty difficult for us to have a conversation with you from outside, isn't it?

Amira   Perhaps Matt doesn't want to be part of the conversation?

Matt   No no, I absolutely
Maybe we should move the conversation outside?

Sarah   I don't think it would be wise to conduct it in front of the children.

Chloe   No, Sarah's right, we should keep it in the house.

Sarah   Matthew! Can you come and sit down?

Matt *flusters at the window, takes one final glance then hurries over and takes a seat opposite the others.*

Sarah (*to* **Matt**)   Finished?

Matt *nods.*

Chloe *comes to the table with a tray of immaculately baked and decorated cupcakes.*

Sarah   Oh my god Chloe. You shouldn't have.

Chloe   Well they're technically for the fete, but there's so many I thought there was no harm in indulging a little early.

Sarah   They look divine.

Chloe *pours the tea as everyone helps themselves to a cupcake.*
Amira *helps herself to two, not going unnoticed.*

Amira (*defensively*)   Eating for two.

Sarah   How far along are you now exactly? I've lost count.

Amira   Twenty-eight weeks.

Sarah   Shut up. I looked like a Beluga whale at twenty-eight weeks.

Matt   You had preeclampsia Sarah.

Sarah   Preeclampsia or no preeclampsia, I looked like I should have been featured on an episode of *Blue Planet*.

Amira   There's still time for me yet.

Sarah   I'm just so excited for you both. I was telling Matt about your whole process.
How amazing it is.

Chloe *and* **Amira** *offer appreciative smiles.*

Sarah   Now, I have got this right haven't I, that it's (*pointing to* **Chloe**) your egg, but it's in (*pointing to* **Amira**) your womb?

Amira   / Yes.

Chloe   / Yes.

Sarah   That's amazing. What they can do with science these days. I mean, isn't that amazing Matt?

Matt   Remarkable.

Sarah   So it's like, it's like you're both their mother.

Amira   We *are* both their mothers.

Sarah   No sorry, that's not what I meant, of course. It's just magical that they can do that.

Chloe (*smiling*)   Well we think so.

Sarah   It's gone so quick. Feels like yesterday Lucas was telling us that Sam's going to be a big brother.

Amira   Yes, *Samir*'s very excited.

Sarah *takes a bite of her cupcake.*

Sarah (*with her mouthful*)   Fuck me. This is incredible.

Chloe   Oh, stop.

Sarah   Seriously Chloe.

Amira   Anyway, shall we?

Matt *jumps out of his seat.*

Matt   What was that?

Amira   What was what?

Matt   Did you hear that?

Matt *scurries to peer out of the window again.*

Sarah   Matt, for God's sake, we're trying to have a

(*To* **Chloe** *and* **Amira**.) I'm so sorry about this girls. I don't know what's gotten into him.

Matt   I can't see them.

Sarah   They'll be out there somewhere.

Matt   They're not outside.
(*Panicked.*) Was the gate open?!

Chloe   No no, we always keep the gate locked as a precaution. They must have come –

Amira   They're upstairs.

Matt   Upstairs?

Amira   In Samir's room.

Matt   In his room?

Chloe   How did you –

Amira   I heard them go upstairs.

Chloe   Oh.
(*To* **Matt**.) Samir knows not to go out on the road.

Matt   Right, I see. Don't you . . . Don't you think they should be outside?

Amira   I thought you were worried about them injuring themselves on the trampoline?

Matt   Oh, well I was until Chloe rightly pointed out that you'd done the responsible thing of having it fitted with a safety net. In which case, we should probably be encouraging them to be out there.

Amira   I think they can play upstairs if they want to play upstairs.

Matt   Of course, but it's such a lovely day it would be a shame for them to not make the most of the sun.

Amira   You don't have a problem with Lucas being in Samir's room do you?

Matt (*stammering*)   N-no, n-not at all. I just, the exercise will do them good is all.

Sarah   Lucas can be very lethargic if he's not pushed. Shies away from any kind of physical activity unless there's an incentive.
(*To* **Matt**.) Anyway Matthew, will you please come and sit back down.

Matt *obliges.*

Chloe   Right then. Shall we get to the –

Sarah   Before we do, I just wanted to say
We just wanted to thank you both for agreeing to
It's so much easier to do these things in person.

Chloe   I completely agree.

Sarah   I mean, it's silly really, isn't it?

Chloe   Well this is what I said.

Sarah   Obviously, all we really care about is what's best for the boys.

Chloe   Exactly.

Sarah   Isn't that right Matt?

Matt   Roger that. What's best for the boys.

Sarah   So, well I guess we'd be interested to hear how
How do you two think we should play this?

Chloe   How should we play it?

Sarah   Well you see we've not really broached the conversation with Lucas yet, have we Matt?

Matt   Nope. We haven't.

Amira   What conversation?

Sarah   I think it's probably just an age thing for us.

Chloe   An age thing?

Sarah   Well they're too young to really understand it, aren't they?

Amira   Are they?

Matt   They're nine.

Sarah   Well Lucas is about to be ten, Matt.

Matt   Still. I can't imagine they really knew what they were doing.

Amira   You mean, we are talking about the same –

Matt   To be honest with you, I'm not entirely sure it happened at all.

Sarah   They said it was a corroborated sighting, Matt.

Amira   A corroborated sighting?

Sarah   I'm just using the words of the Head.

Amira   Hysterical.

Chloe   Amira.

Amira   Two boys exchange a kiss in the playground and everyone acts like there's been –

Matt   Well I think therein lies the bigger issue.

Amira   Sorry? The bigger issue?

Matt   Well, how can we know that the kiss was . . . *an exchange*. As you put it.

Amira   Excuse me?

Matt   Reciprocated, is what I mean.

An icy silence.

Amira   Are you suggesting that our son, our nine-year-old son, might have in some way *forced* himself on your nine-year-old son?

Sarah   No I don't think
You're not, are you Matt? That's not what you're –

Matt   Well I wouldn't have used the word *force*. No, but all I'm saying is –

Chloe   Is that what Lucas said?

Sarah   No. I'm so sorry –

Matt (*to* **Sarah**)   Well you can't say no, we haven't asked.

Sarah   Because we agreed not –

Matt   I don't know that we did agree. I think you made a decision and I had very little say in the matter.

Sarah   Not now Matthew.

Chloe   Perhaps this wasn't a –

Matt   All I'm saying is that I struggle to see that Lucas could have, and don't take this the wrong way, but I just can't see how he would have wanted to be involved.

Amira   Wanted to be involved? They kissed, they didn't hijack a plane.

Matt   It's out of character.

Sarah   How would we know if it's out of character?

Matt   I think we'd know Sarah if Lucas had a . . . a predilection for this kind of / behaviour.

Amira   / Predilection?

Matt   Not predilection, not like –

Amira   You realise you are essentially accusing our child of being some kind of sex pest?

Sarah   / No, not at all –

Matt   / I didn't accuse him of anything, I just said it's more likely that he would have . . . Initiated.

A pause.

Amira   And why is that?

Matt   Well.

Sarah (*sternly*)   Matt.

Matt   Because . . . Just because it's what he's used to.

Amira   What he's used to?

Matt   I don't mean in a
I'm just saying that it's more likely.

Amira   Because we've been shoving it down his throat?

Sarah   This is not –

Matt   What!? No no, that's not what I'm
It's just more likely isn't it? It's what he's been exposed to.

Amira   / *Exposed*?

Chloe   / *Exposed*?

Matt   I didn't mean it like that. That's not –

Amira   Do you think we have him brushing his teeth with buttplugs and going to sleep listening to the Scissor Sisters on loop?

Matt   No of course –

Sarah   / That's not

Chloe   / That's not what he was getting at Amira.

Sarah   I think he's trying to suggest that it's just perhaps . . . unconventional. At their age.

Amira (*to* **Chloe**)   Would you get that, we're unconventional Chloe.

Chloe   Let Sarah speak.

Amira   They kissed, they're not fingering each other in PE.

Matt *nearly chokes on his tea.*

Chloe (*to* **Amira**)   Don't be vulgar Amira.

Sarah   I think what we're just more concerned about, I think our primary concern is actually just the reactions of other people, other kids . . . What with them going to big school in a couple of years we don't want them to attract unnecessary attention. It's already a big enough adjustment as it is.

Amira   Well I always say instead of teaching kids not to be different we should teach them not to bully other children for being different.

Sarah   Of course.

Sarah *hesitates.*

Amira   But?

Sarah   That's all well and good in theory but we can't control other people's behaviour, can we?

Matt   You're making a lot of assumptions here.

Amira   Assumptions?

Matt   Say the kiss did happen.

Sarah   It happened Matt.

Matt   Okay, say it happened. It doesn't make them gay, it doesn't make Lucas gay.
It's just, if it happened . . . it was probably platonic.

Chloe   I'm sure it was platonic, they're only –

Amira   How would you feel if your son was gay Matt?

Sarah   He'd be fine with it. Wouldn't you Matt?

Amira   If Matt would be fine with it maybe Matt could answer.

Chloe   Amira.

A pause.

Matt   I'd be fine with it. Obviously.

Amira   Then we don't really have a problem here? Meeting adjourned.

Matt   I'm not saying it's a big deal, I'm just saying –

Amira   You're sweating Matt.

Matt (*wiping his forehead*)   I'm not sweating.

Amira   Does it make you uncomfortable?

Matt   Not uncomfortable, no. I just don't think he understands what it means.

Amira   You keep saying that? You seem to have very little faith in his cognitive abilities. What does he think me and Chloe are? Close friends? Sisters?

Sarah   Well I don't think we've –

Amira   We all know this conversation wouldn't be happening at all if Samir was a girl, would it?

Sarah   That's not necessarily
It was the Head that suggested it.

Chloe   The Head did suggest –

Amira   Yeah, well, she would, wouldn't she? She's a little fascist.

Chloe   I'm not sure that's fair –

Amira   This is why I sent her the sex and relationships curriculum that includes LGBTQ families and relationships. That's why we have a problem here, because people are ignorant.

Matt   Are you talking about us?

Amira   I was talking about people, generally.

Matt   But are you including us in people?

Amira   I don't know, are you a person Matt?

Sarah   I don't think that's what she was saying, were you Amira?

Amira *hesitates.*

Amira   Of course not.

Chloe   Perhaps we should hold off, speak to the school, clarify some of the details before we start –

Amira   Well we're here now. The can is open Chloe, the worms are on the floor.

Sarah   Look, gang, what we need to keep sight of is, this isn't about us. It's not personal . . . It's about the children.

Chloe   Exactly. It's about the children.

The lights flicker.

Black. 'It's about the children' replays and echoes out.

A sharp ray of light reveals the ethereal **Cherub One***, a glistening nymph in a sparkling toga, extravagant headpiece, with sprawling, feathered, angel-like wings. Their arrival is accompanied by a faint choral rising, the sound of Heaven opening for a brief moment. They address the audience directly.*

Cherub One   All about the children? All about the children, they say.

(*To an audience member.*) Do you believe that?

(*To another.*) What about you sweetie?

You can read between the lines can't you?

You see what's going on here, don't you?

I, for one, am appalled. Appalled!

You know, you work so hard. You put in the hours. You strive day after day to just do your absolute best to try to avoid shit like this happening and then . . . This. Like we're meaningless. Like we may as well not even be here.

(*Shaking their head, fuming.*) No it's alright, just give me a minute.

Pause.

Oh, I'm sorry. Gosh, aren't I silly? You're probably no doubt wondering, who . . . and what . . . and how and . . . Valid. Very valid.

Cherub One *takes centre stage, enchanting music and light signalling their proper arrival.*

Ladies, gentlemen, boys, girls, gays, theys, thems, femmes, I . . . am Analis. One of the ancient celestial order of queer guardians. Thought to have been first established circa nine thousand BCE.

All you need to know is that I've been around a long time, and *this* (*points to the stage*) is not my first time at the rodeo. New day, same old shit. I am very tired.

Cherub Two *descends, smoking a cigarette from a cigarette holder.*

Cherub One   Oh! She arrives!

Cherub Two   Don't get shitty with me, alright? It's been a long fucking night.
(*To the audience.*) Good evening everyone. So sorry for the delay. I do hope you'll find it within yourselves to forgive my tardiness. I've spent my whole evening putting out little gay fires. As breeds go, the queers are awfully prone to theatrics.

I mean, don't get me wrong, I love a bit of drama as much as the next but every once in a while a quiet evening in with a bottle of pinot noir wouldn't go amiss.

Cherub One   Allow me to introduce you to my associate. (*Gestures.*) This is Clitoris. Fellow member of the ancient order . . . and general irritant.

Cherub Two (*curtsies to the audience*)   How do you do.

Cherub One   You see the immortal realm acknowledges that it's a little unfair to birth a homosexual into a straight world without at least offering a few concessions.

Cherub Two   And so we are charged with the responsibility of personally shepherding the queers through the wilderness of life.

Cherub One   Guiding them as they come of age on this wretched planet.

Cherub Two   A privilege.

Cherub One   An honour.

Cherub Two   But the work is not done.

Cherub One   Not yet.

Cherub Two   You see, the moment Lucas and Samir's innocent lips were pressed together, the universe shifted.

A flash of lighting and thunder.

Cherub Two   There was a crack in the vortex.

Cherub One   We foresaw the storm brewing.

Cherub Two   We knew that trouble was afoot.

Cherub One   We've been here before.

Cherub Two   Many times.

Cherub One   And so it's our duty,

Cherub Two   In situations such as this. (*Gestures to the adults on stage.*)

Cherub One   To be on hand to watch over and guide our little flock.

Cherub Two   But most importantly, protect them.

Cherub One   Especially the younglings.

Cherub Two   And, in the most extreme cases, even intervene.

Cherub One   Only where necessary.

Cherub Two   Here they are, insisting it's all about the children.

Cherub One   And yet not a moment's thought spared for the actual children in question.

Cherub Two   Sitting on the stairs, mere metres away, listening to every single word.

Cherub One   Yes, sadly precious little Lucas and Sami never made it up to Samir's bedroom because they got distracted on their way up by the bullshit and hypocrisy.

Cherub Two   Parents like to tell themselves that the kids don't understand what's going on purely to alleviate their own guilt over the fact that *of course* the kids understand.

Cherub One   Anyhow, we have stalled quite long enough.

A crackle of static. **Cherub One** *and* **Two** *ascend back to the high heavens.*

Chloe *pours* **Sarah** *a cup of tea from a trolley prepared by* **The Cherubs**.

Chloe   So Sami says Lucas' party is next Saturday, right? What time do you want us?

Sarah   Oh
Oh right, yes. Well the thing is Chloe, Lucas' birthday party
The word 'party' is actually very misleading, it's barely even a . . .
You know because the house is so small. Just a slice of cake and pass the parcel.

Chloe   Sami said there's a bouncy castle and a DJ?

Sarah   DJ is a bit of an exaggeration, Matt's brother was just going to bring his boom
There may be balloons. Y'know, small ones.

Chloe   Intimate gatherings are always so much nicer. Even at their age.

Sarah   It's just going to be family.

Chloe   Oh right, sorry. I didn't realise. I didn't mean to be presumptuous.

Sarah   Oh no don't be. Sami would obviously be at the top of the list, if we were opening it out to . . .

Chloe   Of course.

An awkward silence. They both sip tea.

Sarah   I just want to say, you know I'm not
You know that we're not . . .
Don't you?

Chloe   Not what?

Sarah   What's the word . . . *Narrow-minded.*

Chloe   Oh well, yeah of course. We don't
Look I know Amira can be a little defensive but it's not, it's just . . .
She's protective. And you know she's also pregnant so everything's a little –

Sarah   Look Chloe, I'll be the first to admit. I'm ignorant.

Chloe   You're being too harsh on yourself, of course you're not ignorant Sarah.

Sarah   No we are. Of course we are
We don't, we don't walk in those shoes. But there's no malice. You know that don't you?

Chloe   Sarah. I think we've known each other long enough and well enough to give each other the benefit of the doubt.

Sarah   Matt doesn't mean any malice either, he's just less inhibited than me. He starts talking, and then the floodgates open, and half the stuff that's coming out, he doesn't even think that. But . . . you have to understand, he's got a very kind heart.

Chloe   Sarah, honestly, you really don't need to defend him to me –

Sarah   We think you're amazing. The both of you. I have so much admiration for you both. For what you're doing.

Chloe   What we're doing?

Sarah   Oh the whole . . . the two mums thing.

Chloe   That's very sweet Sarah. I appreciate it.

Sarah   And it's because of that deep respect I have for you that there's something I think you ought to know. That I feel compelled to tell you actually.
And it's, you know I do feel quite embarrassed about it all.

Chloe   You've lost me Sarah.

Sarah   You see the thing is, I hadn't quite realised how much of a thing it had been.

Chloe   How much of a thing what had been?

Sarah   Well Charlie and some of the other boys had witnessed it apparently.

Chloe   You mean . . .

Sarah   The kiss. They'd seen the kiss at school. He was there. And he'd gone home and told his mum, you know Angie? Do you know Angie?

Chloe   The redhead?

Sarah   Exactly. I do book club with Angie. And so Angie told Gemma and you know what Gemma's like . . . once Gemma knows, so that was how
She was straight on the phone to Louise. And you know

what Louise is like, so Louise comes straight up to me at the school gate, this was on Thursday just gone, and asks me what I'm doing about it . . .

Chloe   What you're doing about it?

Sarah   Yes.

Chloe   About
About the kiss?

Sarah   Exactly.

Chloe   And what did you . . .?

Sarah   Well I just said the school had suggested we meet with you girls in our own time and have a civil discussion, and come to a resolution between ourselves about how we'd like to . . . address things.
To be honest with you, I don't really care that much for Louise.

Chloe   No?

Sarah   She's a busybody.

Chloe   I see.

Sarah   And the irony of it is, she doesn't even know what's going on under her own nose.

Chloe   What's going on under her nose?

Sarah   Look. You know me, I'm not one to gossip. But I have heard, from a very reliable source, that Scott has been fucking the new Reception teacher since Christmas.

Chloe   Miss Garrett? And Scott?

Sarah (*nodding*)   Scumbag.
(*Sipping tea.*) They go dogging every Thursday. Louise thinks he's at Zumba.
But hey, that's what happens when you throw stones from glass houses.

Chloe *nods in agreement.*

Sarah Y'know, she's a full-time mum. They have too much time on their hands so they have to sit on all the boards and make these little projects for themselves and create problems for other people.

Chloe I'm a full-time mum.

Sarah Yes but you're not a dick about it, are you?
This is why I'm a no-judgement mum. I don't judge other mums.
But Louise is in book club, so we socialise. Casually.
Anyway, so she says she's been speaking to some of the other parents.
That they've been feeling a certain type of way about things.

Chloe And what type of way is that?

Sarah The word she used was 'uncomfortable'. She said it made them uncomfortable.

Chloe The kiss?

Sarah I think what she said was . . . she didn't want anyone getting the wrong message.

Chloe What would be the wrong message?

Sarah Oh God knows. Who knows what goes on inside Louise Roberts' head. But this . . . This is the stickler, I'm afraid Chloe.

I hate to be the one to show this to you but I know you'd do the same for me.

Sarah *hands* **Chloe** *her phone.*

It's a petition.

Chloe About the kiss?

Sarah Not the kiss per se . . .

Sarah   I wanted it to come from me because I don't want you . . . I'd hate for you to think that we were complicit in this because, well that's not the case at all.
We had nothing to do with this petition, and as you'll see, there's some really quite problematic language in there that I for one certainly don't endorse.

Chloe *reads.*

Chloe   Wow . . . This is really quite . . . (*she continues reading*)

Sarah   I know.
(*Takes* **Chloe**'s *hand.*) I'm so sorry.

Chloe   Amira's going to be –

Sarah   Oh no you mustn't show Amira.

Chloe   What?

Sarah   You saw how . . . how *fraught* she became. I would hate for her to be put under any unnecessary duress . . . while she's pregnant. I mean, you know stress isn't good for the foetus, don't you?

Chloe   But she . . . I have to tell her Sarah. This is –

Sarah   No but you mustn't. You really mustn't.

The Cherubs *descend.* **Cherub Two** *wheels the tea trolley away.*

Cherub One   It's a brutal business this child-rearing.

Cherub Two (*of* **Chloe**)   Look at the poor soul. Totally at a loss.

Cherub One (*to the audience*)   You are no doubt wondering what it was that was quite so disturbing to our (*placing a hand on* **Chloe**'s *shoulder*) dear Chloe.

Cherub Two *takes the phone from* **Chloe**'s *hand and reads.*

Cherub Two (*reading*)   'Imposing an unorthodox and theoretical curriculum upon the pupils without our consent undermines our parental rights. Most concerningly, the effect of learning about ever-evolving concepts of sexuality and gender at such a young age, could have an irreversible and enduring negative impact on our children's development, not to mention . . . cause much confusion.'

Cherub One *and* **Cherub Two** *share a cynical glance.*

Cherub Two   It really is rather severe . . .

Cherub One (*to the audience*)   Evidently, Louise was not the only parent who bore concerns over the content of such an 'unorthodox' curriculum.

Cherub Two   Evidently, Louise is also a twat.

Cherub One   But never mind Louise, much closer to home, these concerns were being felt in the minds and hearts of Lucas' very own flesh and blood.

Matt *enters, holding a cheap bouquet of flowers. He lingers over his father's grave, then glances to the bouquet self-consciously.*

Matt   All they had at the petrol station.

He places them down gently on the headstone.

Sorry it's been a while.

But, I've been thinking of you. A lot recently.
You know. About being a father.
The job of it. Is what I mean. Makes me think of you.
Naturally.
No one ever really prepares you, do they? They just hand you the baby in the labour ward and . . . Bang. Try not to fuck it up.

Cherub One *descends. As they reach the stage,* **Cherub One** *closes their eyes and holds their hands to the sky, the lights flicker, a deep breath in of air as they take on the voice of* **John**. **Cherub One** *speaks from above. The stage flushes with wind. For the duration of the scene* **Matt** *is completely unaware of* **Cherub One**'s *presence behind him, voicing his father.*

John   Well look who it is.

Matt *jumps out of his skin, falls to his knees, looks to the heavens, fearful.*

Matt   Sorry?

John   Nice of you to fuckin' visit.

Matt *hesitates, then looks down at the headstone where he's laid the flowers.*

Matt   Dad?

John   So you've not forgotten.

Matt   Forgotten? No, how –

John   Well then what have you been doing that's so pressing that you haven't had but an afternoon to come and pay your respects to your own daddy?

Matt   Things have been busy but –

John   You ungrateful fuck.

Matt   I'm
I'm sorry, I've –

John   Very dangerous thing a lack of gratitude. A poison that'll rot you from inside out. Do you know how I struggled to provide for you and your four brothers?

You were insatiable. Guts like black holes. Me 'nd your mam busted our balls to give you the best life we could. And look at the state of me? My headstone? I'm covered in shite lad.

Matt *looks down at the headstone where he left the flowers, quickly gets to his knees and starts brushing it down with his hands.*

John   Too late for that, might as well let me bask in my own filth for another half a decade.

Matt   I actually . . . I came with, with something specific in mind that I wanted to talk to you about. About Lucas.

John   Who?

Matt   Lucas, Dad, my son, you remember. Your grandson?

John   Oh yes, the sissy.

Matt   Sissy?

John   He always had that flavour about him.

Matt   I don't know what to say.
But, funny really, there has been an incident.

John   An incident?

Matt   Or a rumour.

John   A rumour? What kind of rumour?

Matt   Well, it's that he's been involved in this kiss.

John   A kiss?

Matt   Just playground stuff.
But it wasn't a conventional
Wasn't your typical kiss, shall we say.
The recipient –

John   Not an animal?

Matt   No, god no, nothing, nothing of the
No bestiality.

John   Thank fuck for that.

Matt   The recipient, or perhaps initiator, of the said kiss,
also happened to be . . .
Well it was a boy. A male. As opposed to . . . well, not.

John *takes a deep breath in.*

John   Are you talkin'
Are you talkin' about some sort of homosexual type of thing?

Matt   Well I think homosexual is a very loaded term that
implies a subtext which in all honestly I happen to think just
beyond a nine-year-old child, but yes that is the suggestion
here.

John   Right.

John *exhales*. **Matt** *waits*.

John   And you're telling me why exactly?

Matt   Well I
I just thought you might have some . . . thoughts.

John   I'm fuckin' dead Matthew.
Hate to break it to you chap but we don't have much thoughts when we die.
You really think I could care less about who's kissing who? I'm nothing but shit and dust. I've bigger things to worry about.

Matt   But you always said

John   Always said what?

Matt   You were always very disapproving of . . . that type of thing.

John   I don't recall that Matthew.

Matt   Well I do.

John   I don't much care for how you're trying to characterise me here son. I've always been of a very progressive mind.

Matt   You said it.

John   Seems to me a little like someone's trying to pin their own fragile masculinity on their long-deceased father. Which if nothing else, makes them a coward.
If I taught you but one thing I thought it was to at least have the courage of your own convictions Matthew.

Matt (*shakes his head*)   You've just forgotten, or maybe even evolved, or whatever, but you definitely
You were always –

John   What's this actually about Matthew? What's at the root of all of this?

Matt   I've spent my whole life being shit at most things, and being a dad is the one thing I want to try to get right.

John An honourable aspiration.

Matt *paces.*

Matt Look, there's the . . . this rational part of me that is hyper aware that this is all completely ridiculous.
Y'know, if he is gay then he's gay and, well . . . okay. But, look, being completely honest, I just never expected him to be gay. Not to say that I wouldn't love him as much. I'd love him if he was a serial killer.

John Really?

Matt I know I shouldn't. But I would.

John Wow.

Matt The only time I wouldn't love him was if he was a paedophile. Because that's just fucking sick, isn't it?

John Quite right.

Matt But even then . . .

John Even then?

Matt I'm lying.

John What?

Matt Y'know what, I think I still would love him if he was a paedophile.

John Well now, have some standards son. Kiddy-fiddlers are the lowest of the lowest evil.

Matt Don't get me wrong I would hate him too. I would hate what he did but I can't say with certainty that I would stop loving him.
How many men can honestly say, if they were being honest with themselves, that having a gay child makes no difference. Like absolutely no difference. Not one iota. Just from a practical standpoint of . . . you might never have grandchildren.

All parents have . . . expectations. Of course we shouldn't.
But we do.

John   Well all I can say is this Matthew, son . . . Be wary of
your expectations.
We always think we know best for our children but often it's
about who we want them to be and not about them at all.

Black, spotlights rise over just the **Cherubs**.

Cherub Two *does a slow clap*.

Cherub Two   Exceptional characterisation.

Cherub One   Merci beaucoup.

Cherub Two   Truly enlightening.
(*To the audience*.) Parents never lose their ability to surprise
us, not even in death.

Cherub One   Unfortunately, while our Matthew was
experiencing a beam of transcendental clarity.

Cherub Two   The storm was raging on elsewhere.

Cherub One   At the school gates to be precise.

Chloe, **Amira** *and* **Sarah**, *in coats, outside the school gates*. **Sarah**
holds **Lucas**' *backpack*. **Amira** *keeps her eyes tightly peeled for*
Samir.

Chloe   I don't want you
I don't want you to feel like this is an ambush Sarah.

Sarah   No? Then why does it feel . . . distinctly . . .
Ambushy.
(*Shouts*.) Lucas, you've got five minutes!

Amira (*to* **Chloe**)   Samir's not out yet?

Chloe (*to* **Sarah**)   Look you have to understand that Amira
does, she does have a right to know what's going on at the
school?

Sarah   I thought we had come to an agreement. For everyone's sake.

Amira   What agreement?

Chloe   I can't hide things, would you hide things from Matt?

Sarah   I hide stuff from Matt all the time. He knows nothing.

Chloe   Well I'm sorry, I just couldn't do it.

Sarah (*to* **Amira**)   Look Amira, I wasn't, I wasn't wilfully trying to deceive you but these things are all so delicate. I was trying to be sensitive about it all. I didn't want to create any unnecessary stress.

Amira   I'm not stressed. I just find it so difficult not to find all of this completely absurd. They kissed. It was a kiss.

Sarah   Look, I'm trying to stay out of it, I really don't want to get involved.

Amira   Well it's a bit late for that, we're all pretty involved now.

Sarah   I don't think it has to be this . . . this whole thing.

Amira   Have you read this petition?

Sarah   Well yes, of course I –

Amira   And you think this is okay do you?

Sarah   No no, of course, I said . . . Didn't I say Chloe that I absolutely do not agree with –

Amira   But you're not willing to say that to Louise?

An awkward pause.

Sarah   Look, there are two sides to every –

Amira   What two sides are there to this?

Sarah   Well you know, it was apparently also something to do with the books.

Chloe   The books?

Sarah   You know the – the books that you . . .
(*Shouts.*) Two more minutes Lucas!

Amira (*to* **Chloe**)   Where is he? It's nearly twenty-five past?

Sarah   Lucas is just as bad sometimes.

Amira   They used to come out together?

Sarah   Sometimes. Not always.
He's probably just in the cloakroom.

Amira   Why would he be in the cloakroom if they're all
out here?

Sarah   Maybe he's lost something.

Chloe (*to* **Sarah**)   You said something about books? What
books?

Sarah   The books that you guys donated to the school.

Chloe   We didn't donate any books to the –

Amira   *I* donated some books to the school.

Chloe   You
What books?

Amira   Oh they were just
It's really not a big deal, they were just a few inclusive stories
for
For everyone. For all the kids' benefit.

Chloe   When was this?

Amira   After I suggested the inclusive sex education
curriculum . . . I thought it might be good for there to be
some, you know, supplementary reading in the school
library.

Sarah   Well you see I think that was Louise's worry.

Amira   Louise's worry?

Sarah   Oh you know, what with the (*hushed*) *kiss* happening not long after.

Amira   Not sure I follow?

Sarah   I think she thought that maybe they might have been just, you know, emulating what they might have seen in the books.

Amira   Emulating? Is that what you think?

Sarah   Oh well I wouldn't want to speculate –

Amira   Because it's out of the realms of possibility that they might have just kissed of their own volition?

Sarah   Well it is somewhat coincidental, don't you think?

Amira   Not really.

Chloe (*to* **Amira**)   Why didn't you mention the books to me?

Amira   Why would I mention them? I certainly didn't think you'd have a problem with it.

Chloe   Of course I don't have a problem, it just seems like an odd . . . You could have given them to me to take in.

Sarah   Oh God I've put my foot in it again. I shouldn't have said . . . I didn't realise it was a secret.

Amira   It wasn't a secret.

Chloe   I think it's weird that you wouldn't mention it in passing, and if it's concerning our child, I think it's the courteous
(*To* **Sarah**.) Am I not right Sarah, is that not the courteous
To keep each other in the loop?

Sarah   I couldn't, I couldn't possibly pass –

Amira   No, go on Sarah, should I have mentioned the books to Chloe?

Sarah   I was just . . . I was just trying to explain what had . . . where Louise was coming from.

Amira   Please. Tell us where Louise is coming from. I'd love to know.

Sarah   Look, I don't want to be the middle-man, I'm not Louise's mouthpiece.

Amira   Oh you're not?

Sarah   I made it very clear
Did I not say to you Chloe that I do not endorse, I don't necessarily align with her worldview on these things.

Amira   Don't necessarily align but not altogether in disagreement either?

Sarah   No, that's not what I
I think there are nuances to these things, that's all.

Amira   So enlighten us Sarah, what was it exactly that Louise felt most affronted by?

Sarah   It wasn't
She didn't have a problem with the ethnic minorities.

Amira   That's good of her. She doesn't have a problem with Samir being brown, it's just his sexual preference that's the issue.

Sarah   It's got nothing to do with Sami, she said it was the untraditional storylines.

Amira   Untraditional?

Sarah   I don't know if she used that exact word. I might be misquoting here, don't take my –

Amira   And by untraditional she means not straight?

Sarah   Well funnily enough actually, I think her biggest issue was with the transsexual one.

Amira   You mean transgender.

Sarah   Oh is that the correct term these days? It's very difficult to keep up.

Amira   And what was her problem with that?

Sarah   I think she thought the kids might get, y'know, inspired.

Amira   You mean, she thought reading a book about a transgender person might trigger a little outbreak of trans-fever and they'll all start demanding sex changes?

Sarah   I think she was just – I think the phrase she used was, it could lead to someone falling down a 'rabbit hole of gender confusion'?

Amira   A rabbit hole of gender confusion?

Sarah   It might have been disorientation . . . gender disorientation as oppose to confusion.

Amira   What happened to the books?

Sarah   Sorry?

Amira   What resolution did they reach about the books? You always seem to have the inside scoop. How has the Head managed Louise's complaint?

Sarah   Well I think
I think she decided to *temporarily* remove them from the library . . . pending a review.

Amira   She removed them?

Sarah   Just temporarily. Just pending a further . . . a further think. They're going to discuss it at the governors' meeting.

Amira   Oh well that's convenient given Louise is a governor.

Sarah   I'm sure they'll give it a fair assessment.

Amira   Unbelievable.

Sarah (*shouts*)   Lucas, come on! Time's up!
(*To* **Chloe** *and* **Amira**.) I'm so sorry girls, we've really got to –

Chloe   Can we just –

Sarah *picks up* **Lucas'** *backpack, takes* **Chloe**'s *arm.*

Sarah   I'm so sorry, Matt's waiting.

Sarah *exits.*

Amira   What a dick.

Chloe   Amira! (*Hushed.*) People are staring.

Amira   You need to care less about what other people think.

Chloe *clocks the stares of parents surrounding her.*

Chloe   You might not care about these people, but I do. Our children are growing up together.

Amira   Maybe I don't want my children growing up with these people.

Chloe   You know, it must be exhausting always being the most virtuous person in the room.

A cold silence.

Amira   I'm going to find Sami. Enjoy yoga.

Amira *exits.*

Chloe   There's nothing wrong with yoga! You could do with learning to be a bit more flexible!

Chloe *looks around, smiles, embarrassed, exits as* **The Cherubs** *descend from the heavens.*

Cherub One   Uh-oh.

Cherub Two   Trouble in paradise.

Cherub One   I guess there are some things not even a kitchen island can fix.

Cherub Two   Playground warfare can be ferocious and confrontation just isn't in Chloe's nature.

Cherub One   Well then we must act.

Cherub Two   We need to help her let off some steam.

A knowing glance.

Cherub One   You have a deeply perverse streak.

The Cherubs *exit together.*

Chloe *re-enters in her activewear, moves to the centre of the space. The lights flicker as she unrolls a yoga mat, ensuring it is perfectly centred in the middle of the floor before sitting on it cross-legged. She pulls out her smartphone and presses play. A beautiful chorus of nature sounds rise, trees swaying, birds whistling, waves softly breaking. She closes her eyes and takes a deep breath in. The* **Guide***'s voice emanates from the heavens.*

Guide   We're going to start today's session with a guided meditation.
Listen to the sounds of nature around you, and take a big deep breath in.
You are about to enter into a deep state of relaxation where you will experience true inner calm.

Chloe *does as instructed.*

Guide   Ahhh. That's it, in and out. In and out.
Let's begin today's session with positive affirmations. As you repeat each affirmation, know that it is already true. As you speak the words aloud, harness their power, and will them to fruition.

Smoke slowly begins to fill the stage.

Guide   Now, repeat after me:
I love and accept myself entirely.

Chloe   I love and accept myself entirely.

Guide   My worth cannot be measured on any fiscal scale.

Chloe   My worth cannot be measured on any fiscal scale.

Cherub Two *enters, unseen to* **Chloe**, *speaking into a headset microphone, their words echoing from the heavens.*

Cherub Two   Just because I don't bring any financial contribution to this family, does not mean that I am of no value.

Chloe   Just because I don't bring any financial contribution to this family, does not mean that I am of no value.

Cherub Two   My value is priceless, unquantifiable and infinite.

Chloe   My value is priceless, unquantifiable and infinite.

Cherub Two   I am a mother.
Say it with me Chloe, *I am a mother.*

Chloe   I am a mother.

Cherub Two   I am a care-giver. A home-maker.

Chloe   I am a care-giver. A home-maker.

Cherub Two   I replenish the Earth with my divine feminine power-force.

Chloe   I replenish the Earth with my divine feminine power-force.

Cherub Two   My sacred lesbian vagina is unspoiled by the penis of man.

Chloe   My sacred lesbian vagina is unspoiled by the penis of man.

Cherub Two   It's okay to want the things I want from life.

Chloe   It's okay to want the things I want from life.

Cherub Two   Like a big house, with a big fuck-off kitchen island and a garden to rival Kensington fucking Palace. And anybody who thinks otherwise can quite frankly fuck themselves.

Chloe *nods to herself.*

Cherub Two   Fuck them. Say it. Say it Chloe. Fuck! Them!

Chloe   Fuck them!

Cherub Two   Now, take a moment to calm and clear your mind. With each new breath, breathe in strength and exhale all of the negativity from your life.

Chloe *exhales deeply.*

Cherub Two   That's it Chloe, just let the horseshit flow out of your body. Petty bitches are not your problem. Playground drama and birthday parties are beneath you. You will stay unbothered, and classy. You will not let the haters get under your skin. You are nobody's doormat.

Chloe   I am nobody's doormat.

Cherub Two   Not even Amira's.

Chloe (*second instinct, shaking her head*)   Not even Amira's.

Hearing herself, **Chloe** *covers her mouth.*

Cherub Two   No Chloe, that's right. You have nothing to be ashamed of. You need to find your power. You are not Amira's doormat, say it with me, I am not Amira's doormat.

Chloe   I am not Amira's doormat.

Cherub Two   Because you are what Chloe?

Chloe   A goddess!

Cherub Two   And every goddess needs to let off steam in this life. And that's exactly what we're going to do. On your feet!

Chloe *quickly does as instructed.*

Cherub Two   You're going to let all that unharnessed tension, frustration and rage out of you in one short, sharp burst.
Let your body lead you. With me now, on the count of three.
One.
Two.
Three.

The stage floods with disco lights as 'Scream and Shout' by Will.I.Am featuring Britney Spears cuts in at the bridge. **Chloe** *lets out a roar as she goes completely berserk on stage. She jumps up and down around the stage like a woman possessed.* **Cherub One** *mimes using a set of decks, holds onto his headphones as he plays DJ.*

Cherub Two (*over the music*)   How does that feel Chloe?

Chloe (*shouts*)   Incredible!

Amira *enters, initially unnoticed by* **Chloe** *who continues to move around the stage like she's done eight lines of coke.*

Amira   Chloe?

Chloe *can't hear her.*

Amira (*louder*)   Chloe?!

Amira *picks up* **Chloe**'s *smartphone from next to the yoga mat and presses pause, the music cuts.*

Amira   Chloe?

Chloe *freezes, takes a moment. Then turns to see* **Amira***, brushes the hair out of her face.*

Chloe   Hi . . . Hi love.

Amira   Everything okay?

Chloe *nods.*

Amira   Good.
I was wondering if we could talk actually.

Chloe   Yes?

Amira   About this business with Sarah . . . And the petition. Things aren't going to be resolved if we just ignore them. We need to be proactive.

Chloe   I don't see the benefit of going to battle over literal playground stuff. I'm completely behind the principle of what you were.

Amira   Are you?

Chloe   Amira, of course I am. It's your delivery which I don't think is particularly productive.

Amira   My delivery? I'm not the problem here. If you think that woman is any type of friend to you, you are so mistaken.

Chloe   Well she didn't have to give us the heads up about the petition, she could have stayed out of it. She's on our side.

Amira   What type of friend, what type of friend of yours would ever want to associate themselves with someone who is so openly prejudiced against you?

Chloe   It's more complicated than that. And y'know, sometimes you act as if I too am not also a lesbian Amira.

Amira   Well.

Chloe   Well what?

Amira   Well as soon we walk through the school gates . . .

Chloe   As soon as we walk through the school gates, what?

Amira   I'm not trying to upset you but it just does feel like when we're in public round here you're a little more . . . *restrained*.

Chloe   Oh please Amira.

Amira   So you don't think you're more . . . inhibited, when we go into school for example?

Chloe   It's a school. It's got nothing to do with being repressed. I'm not exactly going to suck on your tit in the middle of parents' evening am I?

Amira   No but it's weird to start behaving like we're colleagues or something. Married couples show affection.

Chloe   I mean the joke is you're never even bloody at the school. Which is why it's so telling that you suddenly decide to eat into your precious work schedule to deliver some books.

Amira   It was important to me for the kids at school to have those books on the shelves. Not just for Sami but for the other kids to see other families that aren't necessarily the same as their own . . . that there's more than one way of existing in this world.

Chloe   Obviously I agree. But I'm a little insulted that you didn't trust me to convey that message.

Amira   Well, I mean
Given
What's
I mean
Chloe
Come on
Do you really blame me?

Chloe   We have to accept that people round here are going to be a little slower on the uptake when it comes to things like this.

Amira   Nice people don't need lessons in how not to be wankers.

Chloe   We knew that there would be compromises when we decided to settle here.
We accepted that . . . Six years ago.

Amira   Well you've hit the nail on the head there, haven't you, did *we* decide or did you decide?

Chloe   Yes yes, alright. I get it. We'd all be so much happier in London, suffocating in smog, living out of ten square feet and spending an hour and a half commuting each day. But everyone has to make sacrifices when they make the decision to start a family.

Amira   Not you apparently.

Chloe *is aghast.*

Chloe   See! This is
This is the crux of the issue. You think you contribute more
to this family because you bring in the money.

Amira   That's not what I was –

Chloe   You don't think I've made sacrifices? Have you seen
my boobs?

Amira   You were the one that insisted on breast-feeding! I
didn't have a problem with formula.

Chloe   So you're
Are you saying you're going to
Please don't tell me you're thinking of –

Amira   I'm not getting into that now.

Chloe   We agreed!

Amira   I have to work Chloe. I'm not going to have time to
be constantly expressing milk. I can't sit in court with a
breast-pump hanging off my tit.

Chloe   You were the one that decided one month would be
enough time off. I always said that was unrealistic.

Amira   I didn't decide a month would be enough, our
mortgage decided it!
Maybe if we hadn't spent so much money on the renovation –

Chloe   Don't blame me for the cost of the renovation.

Amira   You wanted the kitchen island . . . We have an
island! But you can't pay for these things with breast milk!

Chloe   You can't raise a child with a cash machine either! It
takes time and patience and sleepless nights and tears and
I've agreed to do it all over again so a little appreciation
wouldn't go amiss.

Amira   Who's carrying the fucking thing?! (*Pointing to her
belly.*) What do you think this is?! This is my gesture of
appreciation Chloe. Nine months and a massive vagina!

Chloe   It was your turn! We always said, I do Sami, you do the next one! I already have the massive vagina!

Amira (*shaking her head*)   This is
We're getting
We've gone completely off topic.

Chloe   I have been so patient. You know how long I've wanted this baby. I've sat out every delay, every promotion, every time you put it off.

Amira   Everytime *I* put it off?! We made those decision together. As a family. And that's a different issue, that's not what we're
My point is that 'friends' shouldn't expect you to sanitise your entire identity, they shouldn't expect you to make yourself palatable to them.

Chloe   Maybe Amira, I just don't feel like my entire identity is that I happen to fuck women. I am more boring than most straight people. Am I not allowed to want boring things? Why do you always have to make me feel bad for what I want from life? Yes a white picket fence, and a bake sale, and a Volvo . . . are all things I relish. You knew I wanted all these things when you married me, and I thought you wanted them too. If I want to be vanilla in my desires, why can't I be vanilla? That's the whole point of equality isn't it, that we can have access to and be equally unfulfilled by the same boring shit as everyone else?

Amira   Only a white woman could think that's what equality is.

And for the record, I'm not saying you're not allowed to want conventional things, or saying that I don't want those things either, of course I want those things with you . . . But if having a life that doesn't allow for any embracing, or celebration of who we are, and yes that includes being lesbians . . . if a life with no acknowledgement of that was so important to you then maybe you should have found yourself a nice man to settle down with.

Pause.

Chloe   That was a low blow.

Chloe *exits.*

The Cherubs *descend.*

Cherub Two   Did you see Chloe go? She's come on leaps and bounds, like she's finally found a voice.

Cherub One   Well that's all well and good but lest we forget, these two are but months away from bringing a precious new infant into the world. It should be a time of celebration.

Cherub Two   No, you're quite right. No greater gift than the gift of new life, and you'd be forgiven for thinking Amira doesn't want the child at all.

Cherub One   Maybe she doesn't.

Cherub Two   You don't believe that do you?

Cherub One   I don't think it's beyond the realms of possibility. And if she doesn't want it, well then we should probably take it back.

Cherub Two   Take it back?

Cherub One   If her heart's not really in it there are plenty of others we could bestow it upon.

Cherub Two   You're quite mistaken, she's just got a lot on her plate.

Cherub One   Well we at least ought to investigate?

Cherub Two   You've got that look in your eye.

Cherub One   What look?

Cherub Two   When you're about to do something inappropriate.

Cherub One *shrugs, no idea what* **Cherub Two** *might be referring to.*

Cherub One *becomes* **Saima***, descends to the stage and cavorts through the space.*

Amira *watches* **Saima***, utterly perplexed by the sight before her. The music fades out.*

Saima   Well give your mum a hug then.

Saima *hugs* **Amira***, who doesn't hug back.*

Amira   You're
You're not my mum.

Saima   Well of course I am. What a dreadful thing to say.

Amira   You're white.

Saima   Am I?

Saima *looks at the back of her hands.*

Saima   Oh fuck, you're right. Well you know what white supremacy's like. Fucking everywhere. White people are stealing the brown parts even in your own subconscious.

Saima *takes a seat and pats the spot next to her, prompting* **Amira** *to sit.*

Saima   Now, tell me about you. How is everything?

Amira   Fine. I'm fine.

Saima   Are you? You seem . . .
You seem a little overwhelmed in truth.

Amira   Well, I wasn't exactly expecting . . . You could have called. Let me know you were coming.

Saima   Don't be unreasonable Mira, how would I have called? I'm not fucking real.
And perhaps I wouldn't have had to just turn up unannounced if you bothered to come and visit us.

Amira   I'm sorry. Things have been busy Mum.

Saima   So I hear.
(*Glances about the room.*) The renovations have gone well. You went with magenta in the end then . . . and Chloe got her kitchen island I see.
Demanding bitch.

Amira   Is this why you're here?

Saima   Don't be ridiculous. You know why I'm here.

Amira   Do I?

Saima   It's about this baby.

Amira   What about it?

Saima   What are you going to do about it?

Amira   What do you mean?

Saima   Because I've been thinking, and I don't want you to get upset about what I'm about to say.

Amira   Okay?

Saima   How would you feel about an abortion?

Amira   Excuse me?

Saima   Before you shoot down the idea, I want you to give it some proper thought.

Amira   Is that a joke?

Saima   I used to disapprove of them too but they're actually very in at the moment.

Amira   This is my baby. And you realise IVF is very expensive? This was very expensive.

Saima   I know darling but we all make mistakes. Maybe you can get some of the money back. Even a partial refund is better than none at all.

Amira   I don't want a refund.

Saima   Are you sure about that? With the money you save on the baby you might be able to get yourself a good divorce lawyer.

Amira   Divorce lawyer?

Saima   She'll fucking rinse you if you don't lawyer up.

Amira   I don't want a divorce.

Saima   Oh now be reasonable Amira. You're not happy together.

Amira   We're just . . .
It's just
All couples argue. You and Dad argue.

Saima   Did you not just witness what happened there? She's gaslighting you. She's not helping defend you against these primitive little fucks who voted to leave the European Union and shop at Tesco. I mean, this Matt chap. Why's he so fucking stupid? Have you ever known of anything so petty? Disinviting Samir from a birthday party because he's a little poofter. As if it comes as some sort of surprise, I mean we've all seen the boy throw.

Amira   Mum.

Saima   Look, I'll admit it. When we first found out about you, your father and I nearly shipped you back to Lahore and married you off to one of your third cousins . . . but we came round didn't we?

Amira   Did you come round?

Saima   Oh now you know we did. This isn't about her being a woman. This is about the fact that she's not right for you. You need someone who gets you, Mira, she doesn't get you.

Amira   How would you know?

Saima   Well I mean ask yourself . . . Were you even the one who wanted kids? Huh?

Amira   It was always part of the agreement, she would carry the first and then I would carry the next.

Saima   Yes but did you actually want this?

Pause.

Amira   What do you mean, of course I –

Saima   Because forgive me if I'm wrong but it sort of sounds like she just sees you as a vessel for human life. I mean . . . Does that really make her any better than . . . A man?

Amira   You're completely twisting –

Saima   You're like her fucking handmaid.

Amira   It's not like that.

Saima   Isn't it?

Amira   I can't expect her to give me a baby and then not return the –

Saima   Favour? It's a baby Amira, not a foot massage. You shouldn't be having it to 'return the favour'. You're bringing human life into the world not trading Pokémon.

Amira   That's not what I meant. We always wanted Samir to have a sibling.

Saima   This one's not even got any of your DNA. It's not even *your* child.

Amira   Of course it's my child.

Saima   Not genetically it isn't. And genetics shouldn't be underestimated.

Saima *pulls a piece of paper from her bra and hands it to* **Amira**.

Amira   What's this?

Saima   It's a cheque. For you. From me and your father.

Amira   What?

Saima   If you agree to go through with the abortion.

Amira   Are you
You're trying to bribe me to abort my unborn child?
Your . . . Your grandchild incidentally.

Saima   Oh good heavens Amira, it's not a bribe.
Just think of it as an investment. In your future.
It's almost unfeminist to not have one actually. To have the
choice and not take advantage of it is sort of an insult to all
the women around the world who don't have that choice. Do
you know what I mean?

Amira   But I don't want to have an abortion.

Saima   Well now that's just the patriarchy talking. Everyone
should want to try it at least once. Like ketamine. And anal.

Amira *holds her bump*.

Amira   I feel sick.

Saima   Mira, darling. I'm not trying to upset you. But we
both know that you're more evolved than this. Small-town
gossip and school fetes? You can do better.

Amira   Mum, can you –

Saima   You're a hypocrite, y'know? You make this big deal
about wanting Samir to embrace his heritage when not so
long ago you were rejecting your heritage faster than you
were rejecting good old-fashioned cock.

Amira   Excuse me?

Saima   You remember how you insisted on wearing that
hideous suit to your cousin's wedding?

Amira   Tarik's wedding was twenty years ago. When are
you going to let it go? I was fourteen. If I could go back I'd
just wear the fucking sari.

Saima   You made us look bad. It's always what *you* want.
What about everyone else Amira?

Amira   You don't get to decide who your child is.

Saima   But sometimes your parents really do know what's best for you.
Just come back to London. It's where you belong.

The cheek of that woman. To drag you to this little Karen of a town in the arse-end of nowhere. Away from your family and like-minded individuals.
I truly fear if I stay much longer I might become nostalgic about the British Empire, and worse, a fan of Coldplay.
We'll be waiting for you. In Wimbledon. With open arms and a bullet for that bitch's head if you need it.

Saima *kisses* **Amira** *on the cheek and returns to the high heavens as* **Amira** *exits.*

Cherub Two *is deeply unimpressed.*

Cherub Two   Proud of yourself, are you?

Cherub One   Oh relax, will you.

Cherub Two   That was undignified.

Cherub One   We got the answer we were looking for, did we not? She insists this is the life she wants. That's a win if you ask me.

Cherub Two   Well while you've been fucking around, something very bad has happened indeed.

Sarah *and* **Matt**'s *house.* **Matt** *sits on the sofa reading the newspaper as* **Sarah** *enters in a flurry.*

Sarah (*panicked*)   Sami has been stabbed.

Matt   Stabbed?!

Sarah *paces the room.*

Sarah   Stabbed!

Matt   What do you mean stabbed?!

Sarah   At school. Today!

Matt   At school?!

Sarah   With a pencil.

Matt (*with a sigh of relief*)   Oh.
I thought you meant like a –

Sarah   Like a what? The boy's been stabbed!

Matt   No, of course, that's awful.

Sarah   It's barbaric is what it is!

Matt   Is he okay?

Sarah   Completely traumatised apparently. Wouldn't you be?

Matt   Jesus. Poor kid. Who was it?

Sarah   Ethan. Of course. I've warned the school about that violent little psychopath before. Do you remember when he tried to gnaw off Lucas' ear in Reception? He's an animal.

Matt   Oh yeah, he did bite Lucas.

Sarah   The boy's always had behavioural issues, we've tried to raise the alarm about him before but you know what his parents are like. Insisting he's normal. Refusing to get him seen by a specialist, and now look what he's done. He's mutilated Sami.

Matt   Mutilated?

Sarah   It was a blood-bath apparently. Poor Sami bleeding out onto the concrete, yowling in pain.

Matt   My God. He's okay now though?

Sarah   The school nurse sorted him out, but from what I heard it's going to leave a hefty scar. Physically and emotionally I'm sure.

Matt   That's awful. That's really really awful.

Sarah Those poor girls. Chloe was in absolute hysterics apparently.

Matt I can imagine.

Sarah I should really call them. Make sure they're okay. I know things have been tense between us all but Chloe is still my friend, and I want her to know that I'm thinking of her. And above all just make sure the poor boy is okay.

Matt Of course, we should definitely reach out. He's not still going to come on Saturday is he?

Sarah Ethan?! Over my dead body. Don't you worry, I've already texted Faye to rescind his invitation. I won't have that savage within fifty feet of my child. We'd all be on edge, no one would feel safe.

Matt No of course.

Sarah The other mums all feel the same. We need to send a clear message that violence like that simply won't be tolerated.

Matt The other mums?

Sarah Yes, we're all in agreement.

Matt As in . . . Louise and co?

Sarah Yes.

Pause.

What is it Matt?

Matt Nothing.

Sarah Come on, say it, what are you thinking?

Matt Well it wouldn't feel right now, would it?

Sarah What wouldn't?

Matt For Sami, you know, not to be invited? Not after this.

Sarah Well we can't invite him now.

Matt   Why not?

Sarah   Well it would look like we were doing it just because he got stabbed.

Matt   I think it looks worse to not invite the boy that has just been stabbed.

Sarah   Oh no no no, they won't want a pity invite.

Matt   Maybe we should give them the option.

Sarah   No Matt . . . It's just going to make everything worse. It looks disingenuous to suddenly invite him now he's been attacked. It implies a guilty conscience. I'll get all caught up in my own web of lies about the party.

Matt   You didn't have to tell fibs in the first place.

Sarah   I was trying to save their feelings Matt! I didn't want to have to tell them that the rest of the mums had conspired to not bring their children if Sami was invited. Is that what you want?

Matt   No, of course not. But it doesn't sit right with me. And shouldn't we try to do the right thing?

Sarah   Well look who has grown a moral compass all of a sudden. The right thing?
You're the one that's had the problem with this all along and now you're making me out to be the villain for just trying to keep the peace.

Matt   Don't put it all on me, that's not fair.

Sarah   *You're* trying to put it all on me.

Matt   That's not what I'm trying to do at all, all I'm saying is that maybe this has changed things. You said it yourself, the other mums agreed with you that what's happened is awful, so maybe they won't have such a problem with him being invited now?

Sarah   Louise is a deeply unreasonable person. She literally cannot be reasoned with.

..se. As the scene continues, **Cherub One** _and_ **Cherub Two,** _in the heavens, start arguing (silently) about what they're seeing on stage. They are gesticulating wildly,_ **Cherub Two** _becoming particularly frustrated and irate._

Sarah   She was saying just yesterday that she made a very strong case at the governors' meeting. She was deeply smug about it all. Apparently there was a unanimous vote in favour of having Amira's books removed from the school and rejecting her inclusive sex education curriculum. Which is exactly why it would be a complete disaster if Sami came now; never mind the kids fighting, it's the parents we should be worried about.

Matt   Well then maybe Louise shouldn't come.

Sarah   What and have Lucas' tenth birthday party be a celebration for two? Do you want to make him feel like he's got no friends? On his birthday?

Matt   No, obviously not.

Sarah   And does Louise seem like the type of woman you want to make an enemy of?

Matt _pauses, considers._

Sarah   No, exactly Matthew. We've not been given a choice. I don't like this as much you don't but sometimes in life you just have to see the bigger picture and that's what we've got to do now.

Matt   I'm just telling you what it looks like, what it will look like to Chloe and Amira, now that he's suddenly been . . . pencilled.

Sarah   It's hardly my fault that Ethan is a devil child.

The Cherubs, _still gesticulating above_ **Sarah** _and_ **Matt,** _come to the climax of their argument._ **Cherub One** _storms off._ **Cherub Two** _composes themself, becomes_ **Louise,** _exaggerated 'Karen' attire, blonde bob, etc. It's panto villain: floor-length fur coat, Cruella de Vil meets Katie Hopkins, cigarette-holder in tow._

Sarah   I'm just trying to do what's best for Lucas.

Matt   Well, is this what's best for Lucas?

Sarah   Why are you asking that now? The party's tomorrow!

Matt   I'm worried it's just going to make everything worse.

Sarah   Well it's too damn late Matt. Everything's arranged. And it's his birthday and tomorrow is going to be about him and we're going to forget all of this ever happened.

The lights flicker. **Matt** *exits. Thunder sounds, the stage flashes with lightning as* **Cherub Two** *descends as* **Louise***. She walks into the centre of the room, immediately owns the space.*

Louise   Darling!

Sarah *is suddenly flustered, dwarfs in* **Louise***'s presence.*

Sarah   Louise?!

Louise   I just wanted to drop by and make sure that recent events hadn't dampened your resolve.

Sarah   Oh, right.

Louise   You're not giving into any sort of guilt-tripping, are you?

Beat.

Sarah   Sami's still not coming if that's what you're asking.

Louise   I know it might seem cruel Sarah but I promise you it's for the best. This party is such a wonderful opportunity . . . It's going to send a very clear message.

Sarah   Message? We're not trying to send any message . . . It's Lucas' day. It's just about making sure he has a great day.

Louise   Oh and he will! It'll be euphoric. But they have to know our kindness has limits.
The audacity of that woman to try to force those books upon the school. Tolerance is one thing, but using our children as

pawns to Trojan-horse their belief-system into our families and our homes? Well that's when we have to draw the line. Thank God the governors saw sense.

Sarah   They're not bad people.

Louise   Ah but now you see this is exactly why you have to be careful Sarah.

Sarah   Careful of what?

Louise   You're like a mushroom.

Sarah   A mushroom?

Louise   You absorb flavour.

Sarah   I'm not sure what that means.

Louise   Do you not cook?

Sarah   Of course I cook.

Louise   If you spend too long stewing in the wrong juices then you might end up soaking up a little too much of their mindset.

Sarah   You mean Chloe and Amira?

Louise   Never mind them Sarah, what about Lucas? Your kids are their friends. It's all about curating their social circle. I mean it's no secret that Sami's a brat. Do you want Lucas to become a brat too?

Sarah   Sami's not a brat, he's a very sweet-natured –

Louise   Don't be fooled! You just wait. He's going to grow up to be just as entitled and insufferable as his parents. Demanding concessions and special treatment his whole life . . . They think they're doing him a favour but one day that boy will hear a no and it will shatter his entire sense of self because he's only ever been greeted with open doors and free passes. They're going to raise an unstoppable maniac.

Sarah   He's not like that, he's really a very –

Louise   Well of course he's like that! The apple doesn't fall far from the tree. They're the type of people who launch accusations, all forms of ists and isms, to try to silence those who disagree with their myopic worldview. The joke is, as if I could be prejudiced? My uncle's second wife was Lebanese. Made a delicious hummus though. Will there be hummus tomorrow?

Sarah   Oo it's not really that kind of buffet. More of a sausage rolls and party rings set-up.

Louise *nearly vomits.*

Louise   You see it gets to the point where you start to feel like the only way you can ensure your child's success is if you adopt them from a third-world country and force them to identify as a rhinocero-sexual. Everything's box-ticking these days.
(*Sighs.*) I mean they come here with their London money and buy that beautiful house and then just swan around like they fucking own the place.

Gentrification isn't a one-way street. The tapestry of a thriving town is a very delicate thing to preserve. Take Scott, for example . . . His family's been here for centuries. They're practically of the very soil itself. We have culture and traditions too, but they never have any respect for those do they?

Sarah   Who are 'they'?

Louise   You know what I'm talking about.
Chloe always seemed so reasonable but it just goes to show you never truly know, do you?

Sarah   Chloe is practically a saint, Louise, truly.

Louise   Just because she looks like us and talks like us doesn't mean she thinks (*taps her temple*) like us Sarah. And don't get me started on the other one. The joke is our children have been at school together for five whole years and I could count the times I've met that woman on one hand and now all of a sudden she's engulfing it like a bad case of thrush.

And the way she looks at me, it's repulsive.

Sarah   Amira?

Louise   I can just tell she wants to devour me like a macaroon. Well I'm sorry darling, but this lady's not for turning!

Louise *saunters out with an ominous crack of thunder.*

Spotlight on **Sarah**, *alone for a few beats.*

The Cherubs *descend from the heavens.*

Cherub One   Well this is just fucking terrific, isn't it?

Cherub Two (*shivering*)   I can still feel her on my skin, I need to climb into a bathtub full of acid!

Cherub One   They're not getting it and we're running out of options here.

Cherub Two   If a leopard refuses to change its spots then I for one am not going to hold myself responsible when it becomes prey to its own damned obstinance. That's on them.

Cherub One   It's our job! We are supposed to be guiding and protecting our flock. Those were our vows.

Cherub Two   We've tried. If they refuse to learn then they'll just have to suffer the consequences.

Cherub One   But it's not just them who will suffer, is it? It's the younglings. Poor little Lucas and Samir. They're innocent in all of this? Should they be made to suffer?

Cherub Two   That's out of our hands now.

Cherub One   Bullshit!

Cherub Two   The birthday party is imminent!

Cherub One   So there's still time.

Cherub Two   We've done what we can. Now we must simply watch and wait. We have to give them a chance. There's still time for harmony and sense to be restored. Have faith, we've done the work.

Cherub One *shakes his head.*

Cherub One   You have always overestimated the mortals. What if they disappoint us again? What then?

Cherub Two   Then . . . Then we can do things your way. It's in the hands of the humans now.

Act Two

Scene One

Amira *and* **Chloe**'s *house.* **Amira** *is violently typing away at her emails on her phone, completely engrossed for the following conversation (NB:* **The Cherubs** *do not appear on stage in this Act until their entrance).*

Chloe   I was thinking maybe we could take Samir to the cinema in a bit? Y'know, take his mind off things. Try to distract him.

Amira *nods vacantly.*

Amira   Mmhm.

Chloe   He's not mentioned anything but I know he's thinking about it. He's been so quiet all day.

Amira *types.*

Chloe   It's all the kids have been talking about apparently. He's put on a very brave face but it's bound to have got to him. Miss Hellier told me that he's not been on the playground at all. He's eaten his lunch in the library every day this week.

Amira *stops typing.*

Amira   In the library?
Because of Ethan?

Chloe   No, this was before Ethan.

Amira   What? Why?

Chloe   She said he goes out onto the playground and none of the boys want to play with him, and he told her that he felt embarrassed to be all on his own. He's been spending his breaks and lunches in the library.

Amira   How long has this been going on? Since the kiss?

Chloe   Well no, apparently it's only been since the end of last week.

Amira   Why?

Chloe   Hayden started telling the boys that they shouldn't be hanging around with Samir anymore.

Amira   Are you shitting me?

Chloe   And then Samir found out about Lucas' birthday party and asked him why he wasn't invited.

Amira   I thought it was just family?

Chloe   Evidently not. All the other boys were invited and they'd all been talking about it and so Samir asked why he hadn't been invited and Lucas said that if he invited Samir the other boys weren't going to come. So then Samir stopped talking to Lucas and apparently Lucas was in floods of tears all day on Friday, and then, well, then we know what happened don't we?

Amira   Louise has done this on purpose, hasn't she?

Chloe   No . . . She wouldn't.

Amira   Of course she has! She's told Hayden to say that. Fucking psychopath.

Chloe   We don't know that, we shouldn't jump to –

Amira   Oh please. This is about the curriculum and the books, she's done it to punish us.

Chloe   She wouldn't . . . not to a child.

Amira   I'm telling you Chloe, that monster doesn't have limits.

Chloe   The worst thing is, he's going to be internalising it all, isn't he? It's not going to take long for him to start working everything out, and what if, what if he blames us?

Amira   It's not our fault how these people behave.

Chloe   I couldn't sleep last night.

Amira   He will be okay Chloe. I know it all seems very intense now but this is just a particularly volatile time but it will blow over.

Chloe   We don't know that.

Amira   It will, I promise. It always does. When I was at school there was this awful clique of girls who used to antagonise me relentlessly. But then we hit Year 11 and I started going down on one of them after lacrosse and that quickly put an end to the heckling in the corridors.

Chloe   Excellent. Only seven more years until he can start securing his safety with sexual favours.

Amira   Look, I know how stressful this has all been. But it's just one birthday party.
He'll be alright, I promise. He won't even remember any of this in a few months.

Chloe   Maybe, but we need to be showing him that he's our priority right now. When the baby gets here and starts sucking up all our attention he's bound to feel neglected. And he's been going through a really terrible time at school, we need to be there for him. Especially today, what when he knows the party is happening. Let's take him out.

Amira   Okay. Good idea. I'll grab Sami.

As she waddles towards the exit the doorbell rings.

I'll get it.

Amira *exits.* **Chloe** *takes a moment. Closes her eyes, takes a breath.*

Amira *re-enters, leading in a very shaken-up* **Sarah**. *She is a mixture of sobs and shakes. She wears a party hat attached to her chin with a string of elastic, placed a little off-centre on her crown, her cheeks strewn with mascara. There are stains on her summer dress.*

Amira   We have a . . . err . . . visitor.

Chloe   Sarah? What are you doing here?

Chloe *immediately gets up, takes* **Sarah** *and guides her to sit down beside her on the sofa.*

Chloe   What's happened?! What's wrong?
Here, take a tissue.

Sarah *takes a tissue, blows her nose.*

Chloe (*to* **Amira**)   Get her a glass of water Mira.

Amira *hands the glass of water to* **Chloe**, *who holds it to* **Sarah**'s *mouth as she gulps it down.*

Chloe   Why aren't you at the party?

Sarah   It's a pissing disaster!

Chloe   Why?!

Sarah *shakes her head.*

Sarah   Where do I even begin? We'd not long finished the pass-the-parcel, which had, by all accounts gone down an absolute treat. Spirits were really very high, and Lucas, I really think he was having a great time.

Sarah *pauses, stares into the distance for a moment.*

Sarah   It was the sumo suits. I blame the sumo suits.

Amira   Sumo suits?

Sarah   Those huge hideous PVC sumo suits that they put on and wrestle on a mat. I never even wanted the fucking sumo suits, I told Matt, I told him that it was excessive. That the bouncy castle was more than enough.
I don't think Lucas was even that fussed about having a birthday party in the first place. I'm not saying he wasn't enjoying it, but he's never relished the limelight.

Chloe   I was just the same at school. Didn't like the fuss.

Sarah   It seemed like a good time to go and do the cake. So I come inside, and everyone at this point is thoroughly

preoccupied with some sort of wrestling tournament Matt
has orchestrated between the children, which, I mean, what
a stroke of genius that was. Asking for tears.

Anyway, the parents are spectating and everyone's had a few
beers and I, as I say, I wasn't even in the . . . I was putting
the candles on the cake.

And all of a sudden I hear all these raised voices coming
from the garden, you know how excitable everyone gets. But
then I hear, I can hear Louise's screeching and I, you know
when you just sense a key change? So I run out because I
think one of the children must have . . . I thought there'd
been an injury but I come out and . . .

Sarah *takes a moment to compose herself.*

Chloe   Go on.

Sarah   Matt and Scott are . . .

Amira   Matt and Scott are?

Sarah   They're going at it. Toe-to-toe, in each other's faces,
effing and blinding and it's all . . . It's all happening so fast,
and Louise is there just barking away like a rabid chihuahua.
I can still hear her yapping now.

Amira   She ought to be put down.

Sarah   And I look over at Lucas and Hayden, still in the
sumo suits, it was Lucas versus Hayden at this point, the
final apparently. And they're both stood there in floods of
tears and I think, this is exactly what I was afraid of and
then, then it all. That's when it . . .

Amira   When it?

Pause.

Sarah   I can hear the words in my head as clearly as when
I just hear Scott shout, and I'm sorry for this girls but . . .

Chloe   Go on.

Sarah   It's not, I'm just repeating what –

Amira   What did he shout?

Sarah   I just hear Scott shout
(*She takes a breath.*) 'Keep that little faggot away from my son.'

Pause. They all take a moment.

Chloe   Right.

Sarah   Now Matt, Matt is not a . . . I want this to be clear.
Matt is not a violent person.
He's a lover not a fighter but he just . . . He just obviously
saw red in that moment and –

Sarah *tries not to become emotional.*

Amira   And?

Sarah   He's not a brute.

Chloe   No one thinks he's a –

Sarah   He punched him.

Amira   He punched him?

Sarah *nods.*

Sarah   And that was of course . . . Well all hell broke loose
then. The kids were screaming and crying, and the mums.
And the dads were all tearing at each other's shirts trying to
hold everyone –

Sarah *starts to fan her face, trying to stop the tears.*

Sarah   Sorry it's just . . . Reliving it all again.

Chloe (*holding the tissue box*)   Here.

Sarah *takes another tissue, blows her nose hard and loud.*

Amira   So what . . .
How did it –

Sarah   Well that was it after that, wasn't it? Jungle madness.
Chaos.
Everyone rushed to get the kids to safety, and they separated
Matt and Scott, and then, Louise is screaming that they're

going to call the police and have Matt done for assault. And
then . . .
(*Sighs.*) And then it was all over.

(*Sniffling.*) We didn't even get to do the cake.

Chloe   There'll be other birthdays.

Amira   So what exactly, in the end . . . Where are Matt and
Lucas?

Sarah   My parents took Lucas, and Matt's brother took him
to cool off.

Chloe   They shouldn't have left you on your own Sarah.

Sarah   No I'm fine, I am. I'm fine. I just. It's the shock of it
all. I'm still . . . the adrenaline is still . . . y'know.

They sit in silence for a moment.

Amira   Can I just clarify something?

Chloe   She's in no state to be interrogated right now Amira.

Amira   I'm not interrogating, I'm just trying to . . . piece
together the full picture.

Chloe   It's not the appropriate moment to be –

Sarah   No it's okay Chloe. What is it Amira?

Amira   Well I guess I'm a little curious as to what it was
exactly that instigated the . . .
The fracas.

Chloe   She's said that already. It was the tournament, Lucas
and Hayden were in the final . . . wrestling.

Amira   No no, I mean specifically, what was it that you
think that . . . I don't mean provoke but what exactly was it
that you think *prompted* Scott to use . . . to employ *that* word
specifically.

Chloe (*to* **Amira**)   What? What has Scott's semantics got to
do with –

Sarah   You mean, you mean the word . . .

Amira   Faggot.

Sarah *breaks eye contact with* **Chloe** *and* **Amira**, *looks away.*

Chloe   How on earth should Sarah know what possessed that brute to start launching slurs at innocent –

Sarah *takes* **Chloe**'s *hand.*

Sarah   No she's right.

A pause.

She's right to ask, Chloe. She's
She's a smart lady, I've always said. You can't
(*To* **Amira**.) Nothing gets past you. You're perceptive . . .
That's why, well that's why you're so good at what you do, isn't it? And you deserve to know. You both do.

Chloe   I don't follow.

Amira   Let her say what she was about to say.

Sarah   I just need you both to know that I'm deeply embarrassed by some of the choices I've made recently. Sami should have been at the party today. On principle, of course he should have.

Sarah *is overcome with emotion again.*

Chloe   Deep breaths Sarah, deep breaths.

Sarah (*gasping for air*)   I know you must both think that I'm, that I'm the most awful mother.

Amira   Sorry, not to . . . but you were saying?

Sarah *clears her throat.*

Sarah (*wiping her tears*)   Right. Yes. Of course. Well you see, Lucas and Hayden, as I said, were in the final. Doing the wrestling.
And Lucas had – and you realise this is all second-hand information – but apparently Lucas had Hayden pinned

down on the mat and I, well I can't tell you why he did what he did next.

Amira   What did he do next?

Chloe   Let her get there in her own time.

Sarah   All I know is that it happened.

Amira   What did?

Sarah   So he's pinned Hayden down, and I'm not really sure on the rules, but Hayden was just, well he just wasn't giving in so, while he had him pinned down, Lucas, well he lurched forward and planted a kiss on Hayden's lips.

Chloe *and* **Amira** *look at one another. There's a long pause.*

Sarah (*stammering*)   N-n-now I know what you're probably –

Chloe   Lucas kissed Hayden?

Sarah   That's what, as I said, I didn't see it myself but that's what supposedly –

Amira   He initiated it?

Sarah   Apparently so.

Chloe   Like a peck or –

Sarah   I know what you're thinking Amira and I'm not casting any aspersions either way. All I'm saying is that I know the facts of what happened, and there was a kiss.

Amira   Initiated by Lucas.

Sarah   I've said that, haven't I? What do you want me to do? Yes! Lucas kissed Hayden! I've said it! Lucas. Kissed. Hayden. Alright?

Chloe   It's okay Sarah, we're not judging you.

Pause.

Amira   I've always thought wrestling was an incredibly homoerotic sport anyway. And I mean that's the irony here, people like Louise and Scott think homosexuality is unnatural. But the empirical reality is that there is not a single species on the planet observed by scientists not to exhibit homosexual behaviour. Not a single species. So homosexuality, by definition, is literally natural. You know there's actually a species of monkey, I think it's the baboon –

Chloe   It's the bonobo.

Amira   Are you sure? I thought it was the baboon?

Chloe   No, it's definitely the bonobo. We watched the same documentary.

Amira   Okay well, the bonobo is considered a fully bisexual species. Did you know that Sarah?

Sarah   I can't say I –

Amira   The primates engage in equal amounts of homosexual and heterosexual sex.
They're a matriarchal society, you see, and it's all about their bonding system. It's their way of avoiding conflict. Apparently, anything that arouses the interest of more than one bonobo at a time, more often than not, results in them all fucking, utterly regardless of gender. They don't care. They literally just shag their problems away. They call it 'scrotal rubbing' in the males. If they experience social or romantic envy? They fuck. A quarrel over food? They fuck. A dispute over their young? They fuck.

Chloe   Are you suggesting we could have all resolved this much earlier with a foursome?

Amira   What I'm actually primarily advocating for here is a matriarchal society. As evidenced by the bonobo, I think we women have far superior ways of resolving conflict than men.

Sarah *blows on her nose hard.*

Sarah   I was just trying to be a good mum. And they're going to paint him out to be some kind of sex pest – she did it with Aaron over the milk and she'll do it with Lucas over this. That woman is a fucking sociopath! She's going to villainise my child, a child!

Amira   Gosh I wonder what that feels like.

Chloe   Amira.

Sarah   No Chloe, she's right. She's absolutely right. I was I was complicit.

Chloe   You're being too hard on yourself. It was Louise that was leading the charge.

Sarah   But I let it happen, I stood by when I shouldn't have. It's almost worse, to watch something happen you disagree with and not say anything.
But hear me when I say this girls, I do not believe – *I know*, that violence is never the answer. I do know that. Matt knows that. But what he said, the word he used
You understand, don't you girls?
That word, that word is up there with . . . I would say it's in the top tier of reprehensible and unacceptable language. The word he used, is in itself, an act of violence, is it not?

Chloe   Unacceptable.

Sarah   And to say it to a child of all people. Can you imagine?
And I'm not defending Matt, he should have never, but what I will say is, I think what Scott did was actually worse. (*Nods.*) I do. And I do not think for one moment that Matt would be the only father to . . . My husband may be a lot of things but he's not a monster. He would not have ordinarily reacted in that way but actions are not without consequences.

The doorbell rings.

Sarah   That'll be Matt.

Chloe   Matt?

Sarah   He went off to cool down and I WhatsApped him to meet me here . . . You don't mind, do you? I thought we should all be here together?

Chloe   Not at all.

Chloe *exits to get the door.* **Amira** *and* **Sarah** *sit in awkward silence.*

Chloe *returns with* **Matt.**

Sarah   Where the fuck have you been Matthew?!

Matt   Well it
It turned out there was quite a lot of cooling down to be done.

Sarah   Oh well I'm glad you're feeling suitably cooled because I've been going through hell on earth over here with these girls. I want you to apologise.

Matt   Excuse me?

Sarah   You need to apologise.

Matt   Look I've already said I lost my temper and I'm sorry I ruined the party but he, he deserved –

Sarah   Not to me, to the girls!

Matt   Oh.

Sarah   Yes, 'oh' Matthew.

Matt   Look. I am sorry –

Chloe   Can I just –

Sarah   Tell them *how* sorry you are. How wrong you were.

Matt   I realise now that my reaction to everything before was –

Chloe   I would like to –

Sarah   He's going to apologise Chloe.

Chloe   I would like to say something.

Sarah   Oh, well of course Chloe. Please.

Matt   Shall I do the apology after or?

Sarah Be quiet Matt! Chloe has just said she wants to say
something.
(*To* **Chloe**.) What is it you want to say Chloe darling? Go
ahead.

Chloe Well, I, as much as I, and I'm sure I can speak for
both myself and Amira here, as much as I appreciate Matt's
apology, if I'm going to be completely honest with you Sarah
. . .
What you did hurt more.

A silence.

Sarah Me?

Chloe You're meant to be, you were meant to be our . . .
well *my* friend. That's why it hurt. It felt like you were
allowing Sami to be punished, and he
He didn't deserve that, he's just a kid. And I didn't want to
say anything earlier because of the state you were in but he
has been miserable all day because he really wanted to be
there. For no reason other than the fact that Lucas is his best
friend and he wanted to celebrate his birthday with him.
And Sami has been completely ostracised from his friendship
group, and, I mean, he was attacked with a pencil for fuck's
sake. No one has stood up for him. Lucas was supposed to be
his best friend.

Amira And let's be real here, if it was Sami that Lucas had
tried to kiss again today, we wouldn't have given a fuck.
None of this would have happened. Because *we're* not
Neanderthals.

Matt Are you . . . Are you implying that, are you saying I'm
the Neanderthal?

Amira No that's –

Sarah It was Neanderthalic Matt. You both were. Just take
some responsibility.

Amira You are equally responsible Sarah, that's what Chloe is trying to say, you realise?

Sarah Equally? Equally?! Look, girls, I made . . . a massive error of judgement but Matt . . . Matt's the homophobe.

Matt What?!
(*To* **Chloe** *and* **Amira**.) I'm not
Just so you
I'm really not.

Sarah Please Matt, why are you pretending?! You had a problem with it!

Matt It wasn't a –

Sarah You said that you wouldn't choose it for him.

Matt She's
She's taking those words out of context.

Sarah No I'm not, that's what you said.

Matt I meant, I meant because it would be an easier life.

Sarah He's lying girls.

Matt Why are you turning on me? You know that I said I would love him whatever.

Amira That's big of you.

Sarah (*to* **Amira**) I know, his own son.

Matt Says you Sarah! You didn't even let Sami come to the shitting birthday party.

Sarah That wasn't
That was because of Louise!

Matt Louise doesn't control you, you don't even like Louise. Why was she invited in the first place?

Sarah Well if you disagreed, why didn't you say something? It's hardly like you shy away from speaking your mind Matthew.

Matt   I did try to say something! After Sami was stabbed!

Chloe   Look, we're not accusing anyone of –

Amira   If the shoe fits, let them put it on Chloe.

Sarah (*to* **Amira**)   What's that supposed to mean?

Amira   You weren't actually even going to tell us the real reason Scott had called Lucas a faggot.

Sarah *recoils.*

Amira   You would have allowed us to keep thinking that our son was in some way implicated in all of this when in reality his only crime was that he didn't make a fuss when, as it turns out, Lucas tried to stick his tongue down his throat.

Matt   Well steady on now –

Sarah   Shut up Matthew!

Amira   It's true isn't it? You'd completely omitted that detail from the story originally.

Sarah   I made a mistake, I've admitted that it was
Am I not allowed to make a mistake? I've said the way I
handled things was wrong, that I was spineless and
You said that you don't always get it right either.
That's why I came. I came because I wanted to make it right.

Amira   And not because you found yourself in sudden need of some legal aid?

An icy silence.

Chloe   That's unnecessary Amira.

Sarah *bursts into tears.*

Matt   Sarah. Just take a breather.

Sarah (*sobbing*)   No, if that's what she thinks of me –

Chloe   She doesn't mean that.

Amira   It's easy to be an ally when it doesn't cost you anything. But you only really find out who your friends are when they take a hit for you.

Sarah   Take a hit? You don't think we've taken a –

Matt   I might be arrested for punching a man for using a homophobic slur, I think it's safe to say that's the ultimate cost.

Amira   Oh yeah, you punched him because you found the use of the word so objectionable. Nothing to do with the fact he was accusing your son of being gay, which, not to beat at a dead horse but based off experience we know you don't exactly take well to.

Matt   That is *not* fair. Just because I didn't rush to make assumptions about his sexuality doesn't mean I'm not in complete opposition to prejudiced language!

Amira   Your actions and Scott's language are just two different sides of the same homophobic coin.

Matt (*to* **Sarah**)   Look what you've done Sarah, you've branded me a homophobe.

Amira   You branded our son a sexual predator! He's nine! And look how that turned out for you.

Sarah   Oh so now you're saying we deserve this are you? Is that what you're saying Amira?

Chloe   Of course that's not what she's saying.

Amira   The universe works in mysterious ways.

Sarah   Uh. I should have known, I should have known that if we came here you would revel in our misfortune.

Amira   You think I'm enjoying this? You think *this* is how I would choose to spend my Saturday?

Matt*'s phone rings. They all turn to look at him as he scrambles around his pockets to retrieve it.*

Sarah   Don't you dare answer that Matthew.

Matt *locates his phone, looks at who's calling.*

Sarah   Matthew Andrew Michael O'Connell, I just told you –

Matt   It's an unknown number.

Beat.

Sarah   Oh God.

Matt   What should I do?

Amira   Answer it.

Matt   Maybe I should . . . Maybe I should find out who's calling first?

Sarah   Yes, yes! You could google the –

Amira   Just answer it.

Chloe   If it's important they'll leave a message.

Amira   If it's important he should answer it.

Matt   She's right, I should answer it.

Sarah   I think I'm going to throw up.

Amira   Please don't.

Chloe   Nobody's going to throw up.

Matt   I'm going to answer it.

Amira   Yes for God's sake please just –

The phone stops ringing.

Sarah   Did you answer it?

Matt   No it's gone to voicemail.

Sarah   Matthew!

Matt   You were the one who said I shouldn't answer it!

Sarah   Well why on earth would you listen to me? I think it's very clear that I'm not good in a crisis.

A notification to signal a new voicemail. They all look at **Matt***'s phone.*

Sarah   My blood pressure.

Chloe   Let's not panic.

Sarah   Fuck!

Chloe   Maybe it's Louise calling to apologise.

Amira   Perhaps you should put an end to the speculation and listen to it Matt?

Matt *hesitates for a beat, then puts the phone to his ear. They all wait anxiously, their gazes fixed to* **Matt***'s face, hoping for clues.* **Sarah** *is so tense it looks like she's being tasered.*

Matt *removes the phone from his ear, looks at it, then at* **Sarah** *sheepishly.*

Sarah   Oh God, what?

Pause.

Matt   It's going to be alright.

Sarah   What the fuck does that mean?!

Matt   Don't panic Sarah . . .

Sarah   Just shitting tell us Matthew!

Matt   Louise has filed a police report.

Sarah (*hysterical*)   What!?

Chloe   Shit.

Sarah   She's what?!

Chloe   Nasty piece of work that woman.

Sarah   Oh my God.

Sarah *begins to pant.*

Amira   Look, calm down everyone –

Sarah   I think I'm –

Chloe   Deep breaths Sarah.

Sarah   I think I'm about to –

Chloe   In for six, out for ten.

Sarah   That
(*Screams, roars even, at top of her lungs.*) Cuuuunnnnnnnnnnnt!

Echoes from **Sarah***'s roar are heard in space. Beyond space actually. Her outburst transcends space and time. It shatters the sound barrier, the light barrier, the Great Barrier Reef . . . essentially all noteworthy barriers are utterly obliterated by the sonic vibrations omitted from* **Sarah***'s throat in this moment. A tear is created in the fabric of the universe, a rift opens and if you were to stand over that rift and listen carefully you would hear* **Sarah** *screaming the word 'cunt'.*

There is an almighty crackle, the lights flicker, it's almost as if the whole world is shaking before everything stills and there is a moment of complete peace before . . .

The doorbell rings.

They all look to the door.

Chloe   Don't panic, it won't –

Matt *moves for the door.*

Sarah (*hushed*)   Don't move Matthew!

Matt   Calm down Sarah.

Sarah   What if it's the police?

Matt   Let's not lose our heads.

Amira   It won't be the police.

Officer One (*offstage*)   It's the police!

Sarah *lets out a panicked squeak. The lights flicker. 'Problem' by Natalia Kills starts to play, the stage flushes with smoke and flashing red and blue lights, as* **Cherub One** *and* **Cherub Two** *enter as* **Officer One** *and* **Officer Two** *in full police uniform garb, sunglasses, etc (their wings remain on display). They do choreo, thrusts, lay claim to the space. They are provocative, lunging at the others, the intent very much to unsettle them.*

Officer One *removes their sunglasses to speak, as they do the music and lights cut.*

Officer One   Do forgive the intrusion, ladies and gentlemen, but we've received an anonymous call to report a crime that allegedly took place at another address earlier this afternoon.

Officer Two   There's no need to be alarmed, we're just carrying out a routine welfare check to ensure that no one was harmed.

Officer One   And gather preliminary evidence to support our initial enquiries.

Sarah   Enquiries? Evidence?!

Officer Two   'Fraid so madam. Evidence is essential to ensure a fair trial in a court of law.

Officer One *approaches* **Matt**.

Officer One   Are we safe to assume that you sir are mister Matthew O'Connell?

Matt   / Yes.

Sarah   / No!

Everyone looks at **Sarah**.

Sarah   Yes. Sorry, yes he is but . . . He didn't do anything wrong. Just so you know.
He's a good man. That needs to be absolutely clear.

Officer One *opens his notebook, gets out his pen.*

Sarah   Yes, in fact, you should probably write that down.

Officer One   Excuse me?

Sarah (*dictating*)   Didn't do anything wrong. Good man. Good father. Definitely not a criminal.

Officer Two   Well I'm sorry madam but I'm afraid we'll have to be the judge of that.

Officer One   Indeed.
Matthew, where were you between the hours of approximately twelve and four p.m. today?

Amira (*to* **Matt**)   You don't have to answer these questions, you're not under caution and you're not obligated to assist them in their enquiries. I suggest you politely ask them to leave and arrange a formal interview in the company of legal representation at a later date.

Officer One   He'll be needing legal representation, will he?

Amira   Legal counsel is a statutory right.

Officer One   But your friend here (*gestures to* **Sarah**) seems so confident that not only has he done nothing wrong but that he's . . .
(*Consults notepad.*) A *good* man.

Sarah   Yes. Exactly!
(*To* **Matt**.) See . . . the officer understands.

Officer Two   Ah good men.

Officer One   So difficult to come by these days.

Officer One *and* **Officer Two** *approach* **Matt**.

Officer Two   But our Matthew, he's one of the good guys.

Officer One   Stands up for what's right.

Officer Two   And against what's wrong.

Officer One   A pillar of the community.

Officer Two   A role model.

Officer One   But we know exactly what's gone on here.

Sarah   What are you talking about?

Officer One   Matt has been a very bad boy.

Officer One *pulls out his truncheon.*

Officer One (*to* **Matt**)   Haven't you Matthew, you've been very naughty.

Officer Two   Someone ought to lock you up.

Officer One   A danger to society.

Officer Two   Punching people?

Matt   He called Lucas a faggot!

A pause. **Officer One** *exchanges a knowing glance with* **Officer Two**.

Officer One   Now we're getting somewhere.

Officer Two *flips open a notebook.*

Officer Two   And yet, it was but a matter of weeks ago that you said, and I quote: 'I'm just gonna be honest here, how many men can honestly say, if they were being honest with themselves, that having a gay child makes no difference.'

Sarah (*disapproving, shaking her head*)   Matthew.

Matt   That's not

Amira   Did you say that?

Matt   That's completely out of
I said I'd love him if he was a paedophile!

Everyone's a little taken aback.

Matt   Also in context.

Officer One   You really are a sick bastard, aren't you?

Matt Hang on
How do you know
That was –

Officer One   Never you mind how we know these things.

Amira *moves to the window, looks outside.*

Amira   Where's your I.R.V.?

Officer One   Cars are very bad for the planet. We prefer carbon-neutral methods of travel.

Sarah   This isn't right.

Chloe   What isn't?

Sarah   Them. They're not . . . They've got pervert written all over them.

Officer One   Pervert?

Officer Two   We're the perverts?

Amira   I want to take down your badge numbers.

The Officers *exchange a glance.*

Officer One   Finally, a shred of intuition.

Officer Two   Talk about getting blood out of a stone.

Sarah   Who are you?

Officer One   Well we may not be traditional law enforcement.

Officer Two   But law enforcement we absolutely are.

Chloe   What are you talking about?

The Cherubs *remove their police attire to the sound of thunder and crackling static.*

Matt   What are you doing?

Cherub Two   We have done everything we can to try to help you help yourselves.

Cherub One   Truly, everything.

Cherub Two   Clairvoyance.

Cherub One (*as* **John**)   It's your daddy Matthew! Back from the depths of the underworld!

Cherub Two   A multi-pronged approach!

Cherub One   We tried our best to restore your inner calm Chloe.

Cherub Two (*as the meditation guide*)   'Just because you don't bring any financial contribution to this family, does not mean that you are of no value.'

Cherub One   And encouraged you to stand up for yourself.

Cherub Two (*as the meditation guide*)   'You need to find your power. You are not Amira's doormat.'

Amira   Doormat?! Who said she was my doormat?

Cherub Two   No one needs to say it Amira, it's fucking obvious.

Cherub One (*to* **Amira**)   It's alright. All marriages are transactional in one way or another.

Cherub Two   And we weren't going to neglect you either.

Cherub One   We know how conflicted you've felt about having this baby.

Chloe   What?

Cherub Two (*to* **Amira**)   We thought a visit from your mother would help you put everything into perspective.

Amira *gasps*.

Chloe   Conflicted about having the baby?

Cherub Two   In all fairness to her Chloe it does all feel a little *The Handmaid's Tale* the way you've forced her to carry this baby.

Chloe   I've not forced her to do anything.

Cherub One   But she didn't really have much of a choice did she?

Amira   That's not how I feel Chloe! I'm carrying this baby because I love you.

Cherub Two   But not because you want it?

Amira   You're twisting things.

Cherub Two   There's no need to be defensive. We've only ever wanted to see you all succeed.

Cherub One   Even you Sarah.

Cherub Two   We thought you deserved one final chance to redeem yourself. We hoped that if you were confronted with the stark hypocrisy of Louise's dogma you might finally do the right thing but alas, you are even more feeble than we feared.

Cherub One   And so here we are.

Cherub Two   Left with no option but to take a more radical approach altogether.

Anarchic music rises, **The Cherubs** *ascend.*

Sarah   What's happening?

As **The Cherubs** *speak the following lines their voices echo.*

Cherub Two   The universe is shifting.

Cherub One   And we, my dear mortal souls, are not like you.

Cherub Two   We have the gift of sight.

Cherub One   And today you will get to see what we see.

The lights flicker and then completely cut out.

The stage illuminates in the glow of a night sky full of stars.

Cherub One   The year is twenty-thirty-seven.

Cherub Two   And in this moral wasteland of a society.

Cherub One   Lucas O'Connell.

Cherub Two   And Samir Rasheed-Owen.

Cherub One   Are but products of their dysfunctional upbringings with deeply flawed parents.

Cherub One *throws off his wings and morphs into* **Lucas**. *He launches himself onto a coffee table, a spotlight on him.*

Lucas *writhes around to a subversive club banger à la 'Gimme More' by Britney Spears or '212' by Azealia Banks.*

Cherub Two   Lucas spends his nights in the comfort of the bottle and his days in a pit of despair and self loathing. He looks for the love he never felt from his parents in the arms of lost strangers who aimlessly search for the same, on sweaty frontiers and sticky floors.

Cherub Two *slowly approaches* **Lucas**.

Cherub Two   Lucas?

Lucas   Yeah?

Sarah   Is that him?

Matt   Lucas?

Lucas (*squinting, confused*)   Dad?

Sarah   That's not him?

Matt   It sort of looks like him.

Lucas *rubs his eyes, surveys the stage. Scratches his head.*

Lucas   Where the fuck am I?

Chloe (*to* **Amira**)   They do share a likeness.

Lucas   Am I . . . dead?

Matt   Dead?!

Cherub Two   You're not dead Lucas. You have been called on by a sacred order to deliver your parents a long-awaited reckoning.

Lucas   A what?

Cherub Two   It's the day of your tenth birthday party. And this is your opportunity to tell your parents everything you've bottled up since that fateful night fifteen years ago.

A pause. **Cherub Two** *exits.* **Lucas** *looks between his parents, then commits. Clears his throat.*

Lucas   You'll have to forgive me if my speech is slurred. I've had six G and Ts, three sambucas and two slippery nipples.

Sarah   What the hell is a slippery nipple?

Matt   That doesn't sound very good for your liver son.

Lucas   Oh you care about my liver now. Maybe if you'd given a fuck about my head as well I wouldn't have ended up in so much therapy.

Sarah   Therapy?

Lucas   I mean, even the most resilient of children would have struggled to come out of this situation unscathed.

Sarah   What do you mean?

Lucas   It can't come as a shock to you that your behaviour was going to have an enduring impact?

Matt   What kind of impact?

Lucas   Not a fucking good one Dad.
It's alright though, with the help of Lavinia, I've been working through it.

Sarah   Lavinia?

Lucas   My therapist. Phenomenal woman, rinses me, but worth every penny. And Lavinia, as it happens, is actually very big on restorative justice. She has been encouraging me to initiate some tough conversations with the two of you, and well I've been avoiding them, but we seem to have run out of road here, don't we? So I guess I should just start at the beginning?

Sarah   What's the beginning?

Lucas   Well some people just know don't they?

Matt   Know what?

Lucas   That they're gay.
(*To* **Chloe** *and* **Amira**.) You understand, don't you girls? When you know you know. And I just knew, didn't I? Well clearly, otherwise none of this would have happened, would it? And you know, at that age you don't understand the implications of what that means but you're just trying to come to terms with this idea that maybe you're a little bit different. And so I cannot stress to you enough how important those initial responses are. They play a very important part in letting you know if you're accepted.

Sarah   How could you think we wouldn't accept you?

Lucas   You don't need to say it. It's all in the subtext. Children are observant. We watch and we listen and sure enough we get the message. And I got the message.

Matt   You're jumping to conclusions.

Lucas   I think the outcome of today hardly suggests that of parents who are at ease with who their child is, does it?

Matt   No, no hang on. I think we can all admit that we've hardly handled things perfectly but that does not mean for one second that we don't love and support you unconditionally.

Lucas   Well it's all well and good to say now, but where were you saying that back then? When it actually mattered. Look how you reacted to the kiss.

Matt   That was
That was nothing to do with you kissing Sami
That was about trying to protect you.

Lucas   Protect me? This is protecting me, is it?

Matt   You're jumping to massive assumptions about why we did what did. We were just doing our best, what we thought was the right thing.

Lucas   Why didn't you just talk to me? Ask me about what was going on?

Sarah   We didn't want to cause you any more stress.

Lucas   Yeah well by not saying anything you said it all. That you hoped if you ignored it, it would all go away. Well sorry to disappoint you, fifteen years later and I'm still kissing boys.

Matt   It wasn't about that! It was never about that. It was never about my feelings, it was about protecting you from hostility.

Lucas   Protecting me or protecting yourself from the shame of raising a little poof?

Sarah   Lucas!

Matt   How can you say that?

Lucas   If it looks like a duck and quacks like a duck.

Sarah (*to* **Matt**)   He doesn't really think that. He's just trying to provoke us
(*To* **Amira** *and* **Chloe**.) He doesn't really think that.
Didn't I tell you Chloe?
I told Chloe I'd be thrilled. Every mother secretly hopes her son is gay. It's like having a daughter without the constant fear of an unwanted pregnancy.

Lucas   I'm not even going to get into the number of grossly offensive implications there are in that sentence.

Matt   You listen to me Lucas. If you think this was ever about how I felt about you, you could not be more wrong. It was about the reality of the world we live in. I would not choose for my child to grow up in a world where people are so cruel to each other. Where there are certain types of people who are not safe because of things they have no control over.

A beat.

Look, we accept that we've fucked it up a bit here. But we're learning. I am trying my best Lucas, but change doesn't happen overnight. None of us are perfect.

Sarah   You have to be patient with people. That's the problem with young people these days, no patience. You want everything immediately. You need to give people room for growth.

Lucas   You have got to be
You know, I'm not doing
(*Shouts offstage.*) SAMIRRRRRR! Can you get the fuck in here now?!

Samir (*played by* **Cherub Two**, *without their wings*) *enters.*

They all turn to see **Samir**.

Samir   Hi everyone.

Amira   Samir?!

Chloe   Sami?
(*To* **Amira**.) He looks like you.

Matt (*to* **Sarah**)   He does look like her.

Amira   I need to sit down, my hormones are going crazy.

Chloe *takes* **Samir**'s *face in her hand.*

Chloe   It's him. Look at him. Of course it's him.

Lucas   Let's not waste all day on the pleasantries and get to the matter at hand.

Lucas *grabs* **Samir** *by the arms, pulls him into the centre.*

Lucas   Let them have it Sami!

Chloe   Have what?

Lucas   If you think I've got hang-ups, this one's got more baggage than a Boeing 747.

Amira   Baggage?

Samir (*to* **Lucas**)   Can you not?

Lucas   Oh fuck, so sorry. Not my place. Right you are Sam. (*With a wink.*) Your turn.

The parents all look to **Samir**.

Samir   Hi
(*To* **Alice**.) Hi Mum.
(*To* **Amira**.) Hi Mumma.

Sarah   What the actual fuck is going on here? Is there anyone else on their way?

Samir   It's just us actually.

Sarah   Us? Are you
You're not
Are you two together?

Samir (*hastily*)   No.

Lucas   Alright mate, you'd be fuckin' lucky.

Samir   Sorry, I just. Y'know, married?

Lucas   Yes well done, do you want a medal?

Amira   Married?

Lucas   To a woman, don't get excited.

Chloe   Samir! How wonderful.

Chloe *throws her hands around* **Samir**. *Smothers him with kisses.*

Chloe   What's she like?

Lucas   Quite vanilla actually.

Samir   Oi!

Lucas   You chose her, not me.

Chloe (*giddy*)   Married! A wife! I knew today would get better!

Lucas   Can we not get distracted?

Chloe (*sheepish*)   Sorry.

Lucas   You see there was a part of me that planted that kiss on Hayden as a protest.

Sarah   / A protest?

Matt   / A protest?

Lucas   Yes! I mean you had conspired to keep my best friend away from me on my birthday. And I was wrestling that entitled little Fiat 500 of a child in the final, and you know . . . we're not stupid. We knew what was going on around us. The messaging was very clear, from the school, from the other kids, from you. What me and Sami had done when we kissed was wrong. And was not to be repeated, under any –

Samir   Can I
Can I just

Lucas   In a minute Sami –

Samir   No but –

Lucas   I'm actually mid-point here.

Samir   Yes but you're –

Lucas   You can have your turn in a minute.

Samir   I thought this was supposed to be my turn?

Lucas Yes well turns out I'm not actually finished.
Anyway, as I was saying
When we kissed

Samir But we didn't kiss!

Everyone (*except* **Samir**) What?

Lucas Yes we did.

Samir No we –
Yes we
Well no actually . . . You kissed me.

A pause.

Lucas Same thing?

Samir Well actually no it isn't the same thing.

Lucas What are you saying?

Samir Exactly what I said. You kissed me, and everyone
seems to ignore that fact and what that meant.

Lucas Look, I can see where you're going here and frankly
we don't have time so let's just put a pin in that –

Samir No actually, let's not put a pin in that. I'd like to talk
about that. Everyone started making assumptions about me.

Lucas I'm not going through this with you again.

Samir I was the one who really suffered. I was the one who
was isolated from the group. Who was uninvited from the
birthday parties and ignored in the playground, and stabbed
with a fucking pencil.

(*He pulls up his sleeve.*) I still have a scar!

Lucas Oh please you can barely even see that anymore.

Samir I was dragged into something which I had no
control over.

Lucas   That has nothing to do with me and everything to do with the behaviour of the adults in question.

Samir   That's not true. You're not taking any accountability.

Lucas   Accountability. What are you saying?

Samir   I was your scapegoat.

Lucas   Scapegoat?

Samir   I was the one who was punished for what you did.

Lucas   You say that like I deserved to be punished? I didn't do anything wrong.

Samir   I'm not saying you did. But I was the (*air quotes*) ethnic kid, the son of the only lesbian couple, so I was the easy target, wasn't I?

Lucas   Oh let's not get into identity politics shall we, those are very murky
We're straying from the point –

Samir   We might be straying from your point, we're not straying from my point. I asked you to speak up for me.

Lucas   When? I don't remember that.

Samir   I wrote you that note. I left it in your drawer at school. Don't act like you didn't see it because I checked the next day and it wasn't there.

Lucas   I did try to speak up for you. I begged Mum to let you come to the party.

Matt   What?

Lucas   She said it was going to cause too much trouble. That you could come round for birthday cake later in the week.

Matt (*to* **Sarah**)   You didn't tell me that?

Sarah   I was going to, there's been a lot going on!

Lucas (*to* **Samir**)   The bottom line is, we were kids and they were adults.

They were responsible for protecting us from this shit, and they failed. And that failure has had enduring consequences on our personal development, and they . . . They are the ones that need to be held to account.

(*To his parents.*) *You* created an environment where I felt unsafe to be who I was. And that's why I am the way I am today.

Matt   How you are today?

Lucas   Lavinia says I have an emotional attachment complex which has left me unable to form meaningful relationships, self-regulate my emotions, and completely oblivious to personal boundaries.

Amira   Well no shit.

Lucas *scowls at* **Amira**.

Samir   Mum!

Sarah   Lucas, I cannot tell you how sorry I am that you feel that way. We were only ever trying to do our best by you.

Samir   Trying to shield him from social alienation.

Lucas   What?

Samir   To give him the best chance of thriving in a hostile climate for people like him.

Lucas   People like me?

Samir   Y'know, to give him the best chances of continuing your gene pool.

Lucas   Sam, what are you doing?

Samir   My master's thesis was on a gene-centric view of evolution.

Chloe (*to* **Amira**)   He's smart. I knew he'd be smart. I've always said he was gifted, didn't I always say?

Amira   Chloe, we should –

Chloe (*to* **Samir**)   What university did you go to?

Samir   That's not important.

Chloe   That means Oxford.

Samir   Now you see this is exactly what I wanted to address actually.

Amira   Was it Oxford?

Samir *sighs.*

Chloe   It was!

Chloe *throws her arms round him, kisses and fusses over him.*

Chloe   Such a clever boy! What did you study? Actually no, let me guess.

Amira   Let him speak Chloe.

Chloe   Medicine? Law? You show signs of an inquisitive mind even now but I think you'd resist following in your mother's footsteps.

Samir   Zoology.

Chloe (*disappointed*)   Zoology?

Samir   Yes.

Chloe   Like . . . animals?

Samir   That's a bit reductive, but sort of.

Chloe   Well sure, it's not medicine but I mean who cares, it's Oxford for fuck's sake!
(*To* **Amira**.) Didn't I tell you Amira, didn't I tell you? I suppose I should thank you really, he certainly doesn't get it from me.

Samir   I hated every second of it. The worst four years of my life.

A pause.

Chloe   What?

Samir   It was too much. I just felt a constant pressure that I couldn't live up to. Like I have my whole life.

Chloe   Pressure, what do you mean pressure?

Lucas   Just tell them Sami.

Chloe   Tell us what?

Lucas   There's no use trying to protect them. They may as well know now.

Samir   Lucas, what are you doing?

Lucas   Just grow some balls and say it.

Amira   What's he talking about?

Lucas   If you won't, I will.

Samir   It's not your place.

Lucas   You heard Lavinia's diagnosis, I have no respect for personal boundaries.

Samir   Lucas, I'm warning –

Lucas   He's been in touch with his dad.

Amira   / What?!

Chloe   / What?!

Sarah (*confused*)   What dad?

Amira   You mean . . . Our donor?

Samir   Let me explain.

Chloe   No, that's not
This isn't –

Samir   Just let me talk.

Chloe   No no, I'm sorry! A parent is somebody who raises you, who cares for you, who makes sacrifices for you. That man spunked in a pot.

Samir   It's not –

Chloe   I can't believe this.

Samir   Mum –

Chloe   Here I am, dedicating my entire existence, my every waking second, to raising you. And it's still not enough, is it? We're still not enough?

Samir   No, actually, it's the opposite! Never mind not enough . . . too much! It was too much!

Chloe   Too much?

Samir   I felt smothered and overwhelmed by the feeling that I was just the centre of your entire world and that if I wasn't fucking perfect . . .

Chloe   Then what?

Samir   Then I'd be crushing your dreams. Like you had so many expectations riding on me.

Amira   We don't expect anything from you!

Samir   Well you can say that but that's not how it felt.

Chloe   I can't believe this. So you didn't like the parents you were born with so you went looking for a refund? For a swapsies? Is that it?

Samir   No that's not it at all I was just –

Amira   Just what?

Samir   Searching for something else.

Chloe   Oh I see. Fucking typical.
(*To* **Amira**.) D'you see this? This is the fucking patriarchy for you. A man who literally contributed fuck all is still preferable than two whole entire female women.

Samir   You're not getting it.

Chloe   Who've worked their shitting socks off to try and give him everything.

Amira   Let him talk, Chloe. This isn't about us.

Sarah (*indignant*)   But it is about us! They're holding *us* responsible for everything that's ever gone wrong in their lives.

Chloe   Exactly!

Sarah   You can't rid your life of adversity. That's just an unfortunate reality of being alive.

Lucas (*to* **Samir**)   Patronising, aren't they?

Samir   Like we haven't faced adversity.

Sarah   I'm not patronising you, I'm giving you the benefit of experience. We've lived lives as well. You're going to get rejected from jobs, and your hearts broken. Because that's life and sometimes it's shit and that's unfortunate. You know this when you decide to have children. And we do it anyway because we want you to experience all the things we have loved and have filled us with joy.

Samir   That's all very romantic and everything, but loving your child is just another form of loving yourself. We're programmed to love our offspring because otherwise we'd just let them die and then we wouldn't last very long as a species, would we?

Chloe   I don't believe that's true.

Samir   Well it is, it's an anthropological fact.

Chloe   Well I disagree.

Samir   You can't disagree with a fact. That's not how facts work.

Chloe (*to* **Amira**)   Well this is just excellent, isn't it? We've raised an unbearable know-it-all?

Samir   / Unbearable?

Amira   / Chloe.

Sarah   I don't agree with that statement either.

Samir   Well please, don't let me stop you from contributing your own vastly misinformed two pennies worth to the field of study.

Sarah   Loving your child is not just another form of loving yourself, if anything it's a form of self-harm! To love something so much, with every fibre in your being and let it go out into the world all on its own. Knowing that there are people out there who will use it, and want to hurt it, and that one day you just have to accept that you can't protect it anymore.

Chloe   Yes, tell them Sarah!

Sarah   Thank you Chloe.

Chloe   You know when you got stabbed with that pencil Samir, it might have stung and you might have felt miserable but I was utterly devastated . . . I haven't eaten properly, or slept properly, or even shat properly since. And maybe that's pathetic but that's what being a mother is.

Samir   Again, just a genetic instinct.

Amira   There are some things science doesn't have an answer for Samir, there's nothing rational about the things you'd do for your child. I'm sorry if we made you feel smothered but that only ever came from a place of love.

Samir   I don't need an apology. I just want you to understand. To hear me.

Amira   We hear you Samir, we do.

(*To* **Chloe**.) Don't we Chloe?

Chloe *shrinks, then nods.*

Chloe (*to* **Samir**)   The moment you were born there was no other baby on this planet that had ever been nor ever would be so perfect.

Sarah   It's true. You look at your baby for the first time and you think my God, every other baby before this one has been a positively repulsive goblin compared to this astonishing truffle of perfection I've just created.
(*To* **Lucas**.) No sooner had you left my vagina than I immediately knew that you were going to be the greatest human being to ever walk this earth.

Lucas   Mum.

Chloe   Children are a manifestation of love. Loving someone so much you want to literally merge yourselves in the form of a tiny little human. Amira is to me, the smartest, bravest, most generous person on the planet. I look at her and I think: The world needs you. The world needs people like you. When we had you Samir, I literally insisted it was her egg. That was my number one condition, and do you know why? Because to me, there would be nothing better for the world than it being full of people like her. Because if we could only have one child, well, then I wanted it to be the best of us. And that was her.

Amira   You've never said that before.

Chloe   I thought it was obvious.

Amira   And you see now that's just completely ridiculous to me because I look at Chloe and all I can think is that the world needs more kindness. And Chloe, Chloe well she's just kindness personified isn't she?

Chloe   That's not true –

Amira   It is true. It's why I chose to spend the rest of my life with you.

Sarah   God she's so right. I have been such a dick and still, still you refuse to tell me to just go and fuck myself like any rational person should have. Where on earth did you find strength of character like that?

Chloe   Samir is right that our children make us behave like complete animals because it's our basic instinct. We don't want to compromise when it comes to our children. We want the best for them and we don't give a fuck about what cost that comes at to other people around us. Even if that's other people's children.

The stage flashes red, accompanied by the blaring sound of a siren. Then two rays of light flush over **Lucas** *and* **Samir***, they look to the heavens.*

Lucas *and* **Samir** *resume their* **Cherub** *personas, reattain their wings.*

Cherub One   Oh fuck.

Sarah   What the hell was that?

Cherub Two   We're being summonsed to another crisis.

Matt   Another crisis? What are you talking about?

Cherub Two   So sorry to cut this short.

Cherub One   It's a real shame. I was having so much fun.

Cherub Two   But you do seem to have somewhat got the message.

Amira   Wait, what's happening?

Cherub One   We'd love to just let you chat to your kids all day but we have other work to do.

Sarah   What do you mean other work? You can't just leave.

Cherub One   Don't be ungrateful now Sarah.

Cherub Two   Most parents don't find out about this stuff until it's too late.

Cherub One   You've been really very privileged to be granted a divine insight.

Cherub Two   Use it wisely.

Sarah   You can't just launch a grenade into our lives and then fuck off.

Cherub Two   Actually, we can. We've done our bit.

Cherub One   The rest . . . is up to you.

The heavens open. **The Cherubs** *ascend, exit.*

The parents look to each other, a moment to take it all in. What just happened?

Scene Two

Lights up on **Chloe**, **Matt** *and* **Sarah** *at* **Chloe** *and* **Amira's** *house, one month later.*

Chloe *reveals a tray of sliced banana bread.*

Sarah   Oh Chloe, not again! You spoil us.

Chloe   Don't be silly.

Sarah   You really oughtn't have gone to all that bother.

Chloe   Oh it's no bother. You know me, I love a bake.

Sarah *takes a large bite.*

Sarah (*with her mouthful*)   Shit.
Chloe.

Chloe   Oh stop.

Sarah   No really.

She wipes the crumbs from her mouth.

Matthew?

Matt   Yes?

Sarah   What is your obsession with that bloody window?

Matt   I'm just keeping watch.

Sarah   How many times do you have to be told, there's a safety net!
(*To* **Chloe**.) He's completely soft, isn't he soft?

Matt   Yes I know there's a safety net. I can see it with my own eyes.
I was just keeping watch. Supervision, remember?

Sarah   What on earth do you think is going to happen to them out there?

Matt   Nothing, nothing.
They're fine. They're just fine.

Chloe   Do come and help yourself to a slice of banana bread Matt.

Sarah (*mouth full*)   He'll have to fight me for it.

Matt *scuttles over, helps himself.*

Amira *enters, noticeably much larger than when we last saw her.*
Sarah *gets to her feet.*

Sarah   Well look at you!

Amira   You can say it Sarah. I'm a whale.

Sarah   No no, you're glowing.

Amira   But a whale all the same.

Sarah   You must be so close now. When are you due again?

Chloe   The twenty-seventh.

Sarah   I bet Samir can't wait.
Gosh it's all so very exciting, isn't it Matthew?

Matt   Of course.

Sarah   Have you got any names in mind?

Chloe   No no we've not made any decisions yet. We've got a few ideas. Done a little brainstorming but we're not committing to anything until they arrive.

Sarah   Absolutely. You have to get a sense of the thing before you name it. Otherwise you're just tempting fate aren't you? If you decide on something delicate and graceful, you know, something like Daisy or Violet, well then they'll just come out a real ogre and it won't make any sense at all. It's like the universe's way of punishing you for having expectations.

Amira   Quite.

Sarah   Matt was terrible at the names.

Matt   Was I?

Sarah   If Lucas was a girl he wanted to call her Scarlett.

Matt   What's wrong with Scarlett? I like Scarlett!

Sarah   I said that's fine by me Matthew but don't complain when she grows up to be a ferocious slut.

Matt   Sarah.

Sarah   Oh please. He's become ever so sensitive.
(*To* **Sarah**.) Now Chloe, are you going to show me this new bathroom or what?

Chloe   Oh of course! (*She jumps with excitement.*) Do follow me.

Chloe *leads* **Sarah** *to the exit.*

Chloe   We didn't go for the copper bath in the end because Amira said it was oppressively chavvy but we still went freestanding.

Chloe *and* **Sarah** *exit.*

Matt *smiles awkwardly at* **Amira**.

Matt   Everything okay?

Amira   Oh yes, fine. Just quite looking forward to getting it out frankly.

Matt   Of course.

An awkward pause.

I wanted to say thank you, by the way.

Amira   Thank you?

Matt   For helping to sort out that business with my little . . . transgression.

Amira   Oh, think nothing of it. Really –

Matt   No but I do. We really appreciate it, the both of us.

Amira   Say no more.

Matt   I got you a little something . . . just as a gesture.

Matt *hands* **Amira** *a small wrapped gift.*

Amira   Oh Matt . . . You really shouldn't
But that's very generous of you.

Matt   It's only something small.

Amira *unwraps it to reveal a small bottle of oil.*

Amira   Oh how lovely, it's wonderful.

Pause.

What is it?

Matt   Perineum oil.

Amira   Perineum oil?

Matt   Yes, you know for that bit of skin between your –

Amira   Yes I know what the perineum is Matt.

Matt   You know it can rip?

Amira   Excuse me?

Matt   In childbirth. You know, because of the . . . it can just tear, hole to hole.

Amira   I'm sorry?

Matt   No no, it's true. That's what the oil's for. You massage it in and it helps make it . . . durable.

Amira   Wow. I don't know what to say. Thank you I guess. That's . . . very thoughtful of you.

Matt *notices a stack of books on the table.*

Matt   Are these . . . Are these the books?

Amira   Ah yes. My lesbian agenda.

Matt   Didn't make it into the library then?

Amira   Louise made a very convincing case at the governors' meeting apparently. Not age appropriate. All rather ironic now.

Matt   Right.

Matt *picks up one of the books, starts to flick through it.*

Amira   I think Louise described them as . . . what was it? 'Propaganda.' And unfortunately the school has Academy status so they're not actually bound by the national curriculum and so they're under no obligation to include LGBTQ families in their relationships and sex education lessons.

Matt   I'm sorry.

Amira   Don't be sorry Matt. Because that was all before. You see once the Head found out about Lucas' birthday party she felt perhaps a little education might be useful.

Matt   She did?

Amira   It probably helped that, in light of recent events, Louise was asked to step down as a parent governor, which left a vacancy for someone new.

Matt   You?!

Amira   Oh God no, I'd rather stick pins in my eyes. No, Chloe obviously.

Matt   Chloe?

Amira   Yes and she was quite assertive apparently in peddling our gay agenda. Volunteered to be there in person to guide the school on how best to introduce the curriculum to the classroom.

Matt   Wow.

Amira   So I guess we really have you to thank for all of this.

Matt   Me?

Amira   If Lucas' birthday party hadn't been quite such a disaster, Louise would probably still be continuing her rule of tyranny. Silver linings and all that. I feel really quite proud of Chloe becoming such a militant lesbian. Quite wonderful. I didn't know she had it in her.

Matt   Well that's . . . very exciting.
Maybe before you take them back in . . . we might borrow a couple?

Amira   You?

Matt   Only if you don't mind.

Amira   By all means, please.

Matt *flicks through the books.*

Amira   I found the one on the polyamorous tri-parenting throuple particularly eye-opening.

Matt *looks at* **Amira**.

Amira   Sounds like an awful lot of admin if you ask me. But each to their own.

Matt *walks back over to the window, we hear the laughter of the kids playing outside.*

Matt   They'll be alright, won't they?

Amira   There's a safety net Matt.

Matt   No I mean . . . What with everything . . . You don't think they're, y'know . . . what's the word . . . traumatised?

A pause as **Amira** *considers.*

Amira   I shouldn't think so.
No more than the rest of us, anyway.

Then, a rumble. **Amira** *lets out a little squeak, grabs her stomach.*

She looks down at her belly.

Amira *and* **Matt** *exchange a look. A moment. Then a sheepish glance to the heavens.*

End.